The Weekend Real Estate Investor

The Weekend
Real Estate Investor

the new, low-risk
team approach
that transforms
everyday opportunities
into big profits

weston p. hatfield

McGraw-Hill Book Company

new york   st. louis   san francisco   london
   mexico   sydney   toronto   düsseldorf

Book design by Clint Anglin.

2 3 4 5 6 7 8 9 0 FGR FGR 7 8 3 2 1 0 9 8

Library of Congress Cataloging in Publication Data

Hatfield, Weston P
The weekend real estate investor.
Includes index.
1. Real estate investment—United States.   I. Title.
HD1379.H35   332.6'324   78-17539
ISBN 0-07-027023-6

Notice

The legal information imparted in this book is in
accordance with the laws of North Carolina, the state
where the author lives and has made his own investments in real estate. Since laws vary from state to state,
and even, in some instances, among political subdi-
visions within each state, the reader is advised to seek
the services of a lawyer when undertaking any real
estate transactions.

Contents

Foreword   VII

One   Basics   1
Two   Your Organization   26
Three   How to Find the Property and What to Do
              When You Find It   37
Four   Buying Raw Land   51
Five   Buying Business Property   64
Six   Multi-Family Residential   90
Seven   Single-Use Buildings and Franchises   102
Eight   Office Buildings   119
Nine   Larger Transactions   133
Ten   Selling Raw Land   143
Eleven   Selling Income Property   148
Twelve   Condemnation   152
Thirteen Going It Alone   159
Fourteen Tax Consequences   166
Fifteen   Finale   179

              Appendixes   185
              1   Partnership Agreement   186
              2   Option Agreement   191
              3   Offer to Purchase Real Estate   195
              4   Agreement of Sale   198

              Index   203

To Anne, my Favorite
MBA.

Foreword

Much of the capital wealth of the United States is represented by real estate. All of it is owned, some of it is leased, most of it is mortgaged. Each year billions of dollars are invested in (and generated by) land and buildings.

Unlike other forms of capital (bonds, stocks, precious stones, cash), real property is not as a rule easily tradable or sellable, and in the final analysis it is this market uniqueness that creates the opportunity to make large amounts of money in land with relatively small—and in some instances no—capital outlay in the first instance.

There are 200 plus million people in this country, and all of them are land users. Each year they use more than they did the year before. The appetite for land does not result only from an increase in population. It comes as well from changing life-styles, producing more households, more roads, more service facilities, more suppliers. Even in periods of zero or negative population growth, demand for land will continue to increase strongly.

Constantinos Doxiadis, who before his death in 1975 had achieved world renown as a city planner, spent much of his time and energy studying urban U.S.A. He did historical demographic surveys, translating the results of these onto maps reflective of the location of our nation's people at given times. Those areas where the citizenry clustered (cities like New York, Chicago, and San Francisco) were shown in vivid red, farmlands in virgin white. The maps were put on slides and used as illustrative support for a lecture Doxiadis gave on occasion, titled "Ecumenopolis."

The slides graphically depicted how rapidly the reddened areas were expanding, extending geometrically outward from their centers on each decennial mapping. Starting at 1860 A.D., using this statistical history and projecting on the basis of what had happened before, Doxiadis estimated that by 2060 the United States would have become Ecumenopolis, one great urban area sprawling over the length and breadth of our land.

One has only to look at the megalopolitan patterns already firmly established to recognize that Doxiadis—barring some ultimate kind of catastrophe—was probably right.

I heard him articulate his thesis in New York in the mid-sixties and was so impressed that on my return to North Carolina, I began looking at my own community in terms of its growth history, noting where urban outer boundaries were when I had first moved to our city some fifteen years earlier and how far they had extended since that time; noting the intrusion of the shopping center on the retail marketing scene and the growth of multi-family housing; remarking the removal of offices from central downtown locations to small suburban units. I concluded that, at least as far as our part of the country was concerned, the Athenian was absolutely right.

It also occurred to me that a lot of people were making substantial profits from these changes and—up to then, anyway—without any participation by me. I was reminded of something I'd once heard a farmer tell my father. "If land lays good and it's on a good road and ain't too fer from town, it's always a good investment—if you can get it at the right price."

I decided to look for some good-layin' ground, on a good road, near town, at the right price but, for fear that alone I might not recognize whether all these ingredients were present, to enlist the aid of some friends in doing so. It wasn't difficult to find three others who, like me, had sensed the opportunities for profit in real estate but, mainly for want of a *modus operandi*, had not done anything about it.

None of our quartet was wealthy; indeed, I expect we were all living on a year-to-year income–expense basis, with little accumulation of capital.

Nonetheless, anemic personal financial statements and all, we decided to commit ourselves to a program of real estate investment, with each agreeing to keep an eye out for an initial market-entrance opportunity. We have stayed with this commitment, although our original group has not been together on every subsequent investment. (What may strongly appeal to three of us might leave the fourth man cold; or any of us might find at a given time that his current fiscal situation has no stretch. Thus we have added others to our list of floating investors who can be plugged in on given occasions.)

None of us devotes himself to our investment activities except on a casual or weekend basis. It is a hobby, and it has proven to be extremely profitable.

We commenced our program in the late sixties. At present we own property which is worth several million dollars. This does not mean—I hasten to add—that we have each increased our net worth by our proportionate share of this total value. Most of the property is mortgaged, *but most of it is paying for itself.* In due course, the notes will pay out, leaving our properties free and clear (and almost to a certainty worth far more than when we acquired them) and us happy and (provided we haven't offset our gains by losses in the stock market) considerably better off than we might otherwise have been.

En route to acquiring our land, we have learned about some things that should—and a lot more that should not—be done when trafficking in real estate. In the following pages, I'd like to tell you about some of these in the hope that you can profit from our successes and failures and in time acquire a substantial amount of land equity for yourself.

The Weekend Real Estate Investor

One
Basics

Ownership—How Come By

In earlier times, wealth was largely measured in terms of land ownership. This was true in England, from which most of our legal traditions of property rights have come, and it was hardly less so in the founding years of our own nation.

Society—even in this country—was structured around real estate. The lord of the manor owned the big house on the hill, and—figuratively in most instances, literally in some—lesser social figures owned the property below, large portions of which they in turn rented to sharecropping tenants, latter-day successors of the peasants of feudal times.

Stocks and bonds were largely unknown, at least until the early days of the Industrial Revolution in

England and the great westward thrust, largely sym-
bolized by the rapid growth of the railroad companies,
in America.

Land transfers were originally called "feoffments."
As Black's legal dictionary explains it, ". . . a feoffment
meant the grant of a *feud* or *fee*, that is, a barony or
knight's fee, for which certain services were due from
the feoffee to the feoffer." (We now use the terms
grantor and *grantee*, and I am inclined to think this
marks a major nomenclatural breakthrough.) Later, as
circumstances under which land titles were transferred
multiplied, the meaning of the term *feoffment* broad-
ened and it came to characterize any conveyance of
real estate. Title to land was referred to as "seisin"
and was passed from one to another through the
process of "livery of seisin" which, in ancient times,
involved a visit by—permit me—grantor and grantee
to the premises and a symbolic handing over of some
appurtenance: a branch, a twig, a handful of dirt, a
key.

While the word *feoffment* has passed into disuse,
many common-law legal terms affecting real property
are still used. For example, *fee* remains the generic
term for land title. If you own land, you hold the fee
and your title is described as one of fee simple or fee
simple absolute. From the word *seisin*, we draw the
participial pronouncement that one is "seized," that is,
holds title to, the premises, and this phrasing frequently
appears today in documents of conveyance. Grantor
warrants that he is seized of the premises and has the
right to convey the same and that he will warrant and
defend the title against all comers.

The act of going on property for the title-passing
ceremony was sometimes referred to as the "deed" of
transfer, and so the word *deed* has been carried

forward to describe the paper writing which is now used to pass title. Unless you inherit land, you acquire it by deed.

Of course, nowadays you don't have to go near the property to effect a change of ownership. The owner prepares and delivers a deed to you. This document contains the names of the parties, a description of the property, and appropriate language of conveyance, and upon delivery, passes the title.

Under our system, all land is owned, all the time. As the phrase goes, "There is never a gap or lap in the seisin." If you die intestate (without a will), the law fictionalizes that even as you are taking that last, precious breath, title to your real estate is magically springing to your next of kin. If you die testate (with a will), it moves just as rapidly to your devisees (testamentary recipients of real estate).

Ownership—Records of

The business of tracking the myriad transactions affecting land titles is largely in the hands of registers of deeds (in whose offices, county by county, all real property documents are—or should be—recorded); clerks of court (in whose offices all court proceedings which might affect land titles are matters of record); and tax collectors and supervisors (in whose offices all land—even that owned by charitable and other non-taxable institutions—is mapped and listed).

As you can imagine, orderly record keeping of land ownership is a difficult and complex task, particularly in heavily populated areas.

Your deed will not be recorded unless you take it to the recording office and request that it be entered in the public registry. Usually this is done at the time real estate transactions are consummated, more often than not by a lawyer in attendance at the closing.

Failure to record your deed does not diminish your title. However, if your grantor later deeds the same property to another party, and *that* grantee records *his* deed, before you have recorded yours, he then holds the title to this real estate, good against the world, and the world includes you. In some states this proposition holds even where such subsequent grantee is aware of the earlier, unrecorded conveyance. You, as the slothful first owner, would only have a right against your original grantor for damages, and the value of that right, realistically speaking, would depend on whether you could still find this party and whether, if and when you did, he was solvent.

Advisory: Always record your deed immediately.

What has been said about recording deeds applies with equal force to the recording of mortgages or other security instruments creating a lien on the land. In some states, instruments performing the function of a mortgage are referred to as deeds of trust; foreclosure procedures under the latter are slightly different, but substantively the documents perform the same function. A mortgage, of course, is a paper writing given by buyer to seller—or to a third-party lender—authorizing the mortgagee to sell the property described therein at public auction *if* the mortgagor fails to pay his debt to mortgagee on schedule.

So long as the debt secured by the mortgage remains unpaid, the public record will reflect that you're still in hock. However, when you've finally paid it off, you may take the canceled original note and mortgage to the register of deeds, who will then note, on the record, that your property is now debt-free.

As well as deeds and mortgages, other documents

and transactions that might affect title to real estate are spread on the public record. Judgments and tax liens and incompetency proceedings are examples of these. Because of all this, an attorney can give you assurance that you will (or in some instances won't) be able to acquire a good title to the property of your choice.

Title Search—Importance of

At the outset, I urge you to recognize the importance of title search. *Don't ever buy a piece of land without first having its history searched and its title certified by title counsel.* If the transaction is large enough, you should also obtain (in many instances, your lender will insist you obtain) title insurance. You may be dealing with the most reputable of sellers, but a grantor's personal assurance that the title is defect-free will not help you if it turns out that he's wrong. True, you will probably have received a warranty deed and thus will be able to go back against the seller for any damages you may sustain, but this will be at best an expensive inconvenience and at worst the glowing plans you had for your new property will be substantially delayed, perhaps ultimately defeated. So why chance it?

Uniqueness and Financeability

Now let's look at some of land's unique characteristics as an investment vehicle. Most of them are obvious, but sometimes it's the obvious that is overlooked.

It is true that land can be made. The most spectacular example of this, of course, is provided by the creation narrative in Genesis I. Lesser, later additions to the earth's surface have been made possible through the ingenuity of engineers in Monaco and Fort Lauderdale, among other places (dredging dirt from the deep and stacking it in the shallows). Nevertheless, and all of this notwithstanding, I think we can safely assert that in general we are dealing with a fixed, known, positioned supply.

More land is required for public and private use each day. Thus we can say that we are dealing with a constantly diminishing supply and an ever-increasing demand.

Primarily for the foregoing reasons, land is more financeable than any other form of capital. Financing may be accomplished in various ways (we will discuss some of these later, in detail). Generally, one borrows from a licensed lender or gives a note for the deferred balance of initial cost to the seller. It is possible and legally permissible to borrow up to 100 percent of the cost of land.

Indeed, in real estate investment, financing is the name of the game. You will see that even in the comparatively modest kinds of acquisitions we will be discussing in succeeding chapters, considerable monies—and thus obligations—will be involved. Because of this I offer a word of caution, even admonition, at the outset: If debt per se tends to bother you unduly (as opposed to, say, duly), then real estate investment is not for you.

This word of warning has special application, in fact, because in the course of this book I will be advising you not only to buy land but also to continuously expand your holdings. The basic premise of building your own small real estate empire is pyramiding, using every purchase to help with the next one and continuing to buy, whatever else betides. The proceeds of an occasional sale should be used to pay any debts that must currently be met and then applied to the acquisition of additional property as something worthwhile becomes available.

Even more important, as we shall see, you should always seek to avoid situations where you *have* to sell. I suppose a corollary of this is that you should search diligently for those owners of real property who haven't been prudent enough to realize this.

Marketing Advantages and Disadvantages

There is no central marketplace for land, no New York or Pacific Coast or Chicago Land Exchange; no gathering point, where buyers and sellers congregate regularly to establish prices based on the ebb and flow of the marketplace. Neither is there a Federal Land Exchange Commission to regulate sales and financing (margin) requirements. The reasons are obvious enough. Land is not fungible. Every piece is different. Laws regulating the validity of conveyances vary from state to state. Land cannot be transported. There are no maximums and no minimums, no askeds, or bids. Its price is what its owner says it is, which in the final analysis, is what he will take for it.

The courts have forever judicially defined the fair market value of land as that price which a seller who is willing but not compelled to sell and a buyer who is willing but not compelled to buy can agree on. It's an illusory standard, that one, and rarely if ever enters the minds of bargainers in individual transactions. "What'll you take?" and "What'll you give?" are the questions, and while this simplified statement of the bargaining start-up point can be said to apply to the most complex of purchase and sale transactions, in no other bargaining arena that I know does it occur in so simple and stark an encounter as between seller and buyer of real estate.

Of course, as is the case with most pluses in life, there is a correlative minus to the plus of nonregulation in the real estate market. You may at any given time have difficulty finding a buyer for your property. Thus, if quick liquidity is a main mission of your investment program, stay away from land. Even for good income-producing property, buyers will not always be available, at least on short notice and at your price.

Non–Income-Producing Land

Just as a general investment program should not be exclusively concentrated in one kind of security, so your real estate acquisitions should not be exclusively of non–income-producing (or income-producing) land.

The advantages and disadvantages of each form are apparent, but some of them might bear listing for emphasis.

We know, for example, that raw land tends to have more market volatility than land with buildings already on it. Values can be affected dramatically by such things as zoning change, neighborhood character change, the unpredicted and unpredictable decision to locate some major enterprise close to your land (a shopping mall, for example, or a manufacturing plant), the vicissitudes of the general marketplace, the location or widening of a nearby road. *The long-term trend of land values is always up,* and, even in the absence of traumatic and evident neighborhood changes, this axiomatic proposition will always be working for you, usually at a more rapid rate in the case of unimproved property. Real estate markets, however, like all other markets, are subject to occasional depression, and you must at least anticipate that your land could become less valuable than it was when you bought it. This possibility provides one reason among many why you should never be so obligated with land purchase commitments that you might foreseeably have to liquidate your holdings, or some of them, suddenly. There is very little point in planting a crop that you might not be around to harvest.

Raw land tends to be harder to dispose of than income property. Most people buy property to meet a specific, immediate need, not to hold against appreciation possibilities or against the chance that someone might want all or some of it and will be willing to pay a handsome profit to the owner in exchange for a deed. It is when the needs of some prowling purchaser coincide with the location and availability of your property that your initial foresight in acquiring it will be rewarded.

Five years ago our group (we'll discuss the legal and philosophical concept of group action in acquiring property later) purchased a 50-acre tract of land which we felt had good long-range potential. In the intervening period, a number of developments in the immediate vicinity have heightened this property's value considerably, and recently we sold 10 of the 50 acres for exactly the same amount we paid for the total tract initially. Thus, at the moment, our investment in the land amounts to no more than the money we've spent for *ad valorem* taxes (as annual city or county property assessments are usually called) and interest, both of which expenses have been deductible and have therefore only cost us a net of our tax-bracket level subtracted from 100 (if you are in a 30-percent tax bracket, for example, your interest cost nets out at 70 percent of the amount actually paid).

We still have 40 acres remaining, and its value will be further increased by the apartments which the purchaser of the 10 acres proposes to construct on the property.

Had we been forced to put this land on the block, however, to sell at the best price we could get within a short time, it is quite possible that we might not have realized any profit at all.

Remember always that with respect to any land you own, the government permits you to perform monopolistically. You, and you alone, control whatever portion of the planet your property occupies. You cannot be forced to sell, and you alone set the price. If your land is well situated, sooner or later someone will want to buy it, and its value will not be what comparable land is generally selling for in the marketplace, *but rather, what that particular location (the only one like it in your community) is worth to such purchaser for the particular use proposed for it.*

As we will see by reference to specific examples in a later chapter, non–income-producing land can normally be purchased under more flexible financing arrangements and affords a wider range in price negotiation than is the case with its revenue-productive counterpart.

When you buy raw land, without planning to develop it yourself (as you will shortly see, I strongly advocate that you stay away from that kind of entrepreneurial involvement), you are speculating in two things primarily. You have calculated on the basis of history's teaching, as well as on the basis of demand and supply, that the land will grow in value at such a speed as to outdistance its carrying costs (i.e., and primarily, interest and taxes). You may also have a plan for selling off sections of the property and recovering total purchase cost in the short run by this method, leaving the remainder of the property yours cost-free, to be held or sold at your leisure.

Pricing raw land is not easy, particularly where it is just beyond suburban development. It may or may not have easy access to water or sewer services (a check with your city or county water and sewer department will inform you). It may border on a rail line, giving it additional industrial potential, or have excellent access to an interstate highway. It may be relatively level or topographically difficult. It may be zoned as farmland or as a single-family residential area or for industry, or it may not be zoned at all, in which case it can legally be put to any use. Your city or county planning and zoning office will be able to provide you with comprehensive, current information on these points and will normally have available manuals explaining the particular limitations of each zoning category.

Some of the property might be in floodplain, meaning that its building-site potential is reduced or limited because of its susceptibility to flooding in times of heavy rainfall (again, this determination has probably been made by your local planning office, with which you should always check in advance of purchase negotiations).

As a rule, the bigger the tract, the cheaper the price per acre. Thus, if land across the road sold for $3,000 an acre in a 10-acre tract, and yours is a 100-acre farm, the 10-acre sale would not be a recognized comparable in the eyes of most appraisers. On the other hand, it is an indication of recent interest in the location and thus supportive of your own.

Income-Producing Land

For openers, income property is another and vastly different kettle of fish as compared with non–income-producing land. Value becomes much less speculative, since you're now dealing with a present, calculable return on investment. You are also dealing with leases of varying durations, rents with variables (e.g., percentage of sales revenue against a minimum fixed rental), depreciation (raw land, because of its very nature, is not depreciable, but all improvements placed on land may be depreciated), and many other factors, most of which we will discuss later.

Not surprisingly, income-producing property tends to have relatively stable value, particularly if rents are not subject to heavy fluctuation (as from seasonal demand change in the case of residential property or mercurial sales-percentage overrides in the case of business property). There is a reasonably predictable return, and the primary bargaining differentials are introduced by seller's position (he may have used up his depreciation benefits or, as might be the case in any buy-sell situation, simply have an urgent need to cash in his chips) and, of course, the intensity of buyer's desire to acquire the property. Buyer may be desperately in need of some tax shelter and thus be willing to pay slightly more than the property is worth on a strict economic-return basis. Later, we will look more closely at both sides of this bargaining coin where income property is involved.

Of course, rent-producing land tends to be easier to dispose of. Not easy. Just easier.

Income property has automatic equity buildup via automatic debt liquidation. The rent makes the mortgage payments. *This is the single most important fact to remember about income-producing real estate, and*

*this is what distinguishes it from most other invest-
ments.* If you finance the purchase of a valuable piece
of jewelry, you make your down payment and then
hope you can come up with the balance at the appropriate times. If you buy stocks or bonds on margin,
you must come up with the equity investment from
some source or other when you buy the securities. But
when you finance income real estate, the property in
large measure pays for itself. Not only does it pay for
itself, but through depreciation and other allowable
expense deductions, it also permits you to get a return
of some or all of this investment tax-free. Moreover, in
contradistinction to leaseable personal property (e.g.,
autos, computers), the passage of time tends to make
land more, rather than less, valuable. Later we will
apply various financing techniques to specific types of
cases. For now, I will only note that arranging long-
term financing (the kind you will usually need) for
income property is quite a different undertaking from
negotiating a purchase-money loan with Farmer
Brown on that acreage tract you are buying from him,
or even a short-term loan on raw land from your local
banker.

For income-producing property, you might find a
range in loan terms of from fifteen to twenty-five years;
a difference in interest rates of from .5 to 1.5 percent;
in points (premium paid to the broker or lender at the
time of loan closing), of from 1 to 2 percent (of total
loan commitment); and in percent of purchase price
loanable, of from 60 to 80 percent. With some lending
institutions (particularly savings and loans), you might
be able to improve the percent of purchase price
loaned by purchasing mortgage guaranty insurance
(under terms whereby the insurer guarantees the
lender against any default by you on the insured
portion of the loan balance, e.g., the top 20 percent).

Of course, there will often be instances where you can purchase income-producing property without long-term financing by a lending institution. We will shortly mention one example of this and will subsequently discuss others in depth. The possibility of purchase-money (i.e., seller) financing should always be explored, for, all things considered, it usually proves to be the best kind of all.

You will buy what is generically called business property or you will buy an apartment project. In the case of the former, you will normally, as a casual investor, be involved with retail business enterprise as opposed to, say, a warehouse or manufacturing plant. In the case of the latter, an apartment is an apartment is an apartment. With respect to both, there are signs of sickness and health of which you will need to be aware, and in the course of this study we will mention many of them.

Finding business properties suitable to your needs is never easy. By and large, you will have a better chance with an older tract—something that has been around for ten or fifteen years. This is so because the owner will have eaten into his shelter benefits so heavily that he may be losing the tax-free cash-flow factor which enticed him into the investment in the first place.

Let me offer a preliminary skeleton comment on tax shelter at this point and then later put some flesh on it. Notwithstanding evidence to the contrary offered by certain Greek and Roman edifices, buildings do not last forever, at least from a functional standpoint. Our government, so lacking in understanding in many areas, comprehends this and thus allows an owner of business property to recover the cost of his building tax-free. Since these taxes are paid annually, an annual rate of depreciation is permitted. For example, if your building has an estimated remaining life (the IRS and your accountant have tables to ease the burden of making this calculation) of twenty-five years when you acquire it, you take 4 percent of its purchase price each year as recovery of your cost—or, to put it another way, as return of your capital. The rationale is that you will then use this freed money as a building fund for a new structure. However, you do not have to employ it—or make any legal or moral commitment to employ it—in this fashion. Since depreciation is treated as an expense (just like maintenance and insurance) for tax purposes, the figure of 4 percent in our hypothetical case becomes a deductible item—*even though you have not actually paid it to anyone.* You may thus have a net plus cash flow from your rent collections and a tax loss.

Now, returning to our comment that available properties will normally be ten to fifteen years old, I will add a further qualifier. Until recently, one could accelerate his depreciation with respect to any kind of property. This acceleration permissiveness has now been narrowed considerably, but it was probably in effect when the structure you are looking at was built and its owner just as probably took advantage of it. Accelerated depreciation, as the term suggests, permitted faster write-off. Unfortunately for the one who opted for this alternative, it did not permit shortened building-life estimates. Rather, under different formulas, it provided for heavy depreciation in the early years, leveling off and easing into very light depreciation in the later ones. Thus, the owner of property which has attracted your interest, if he has used an accelerated schedule, may be particularly anxious to unload his land, especially if he is in a high tax bracket.

In this connection, please note that business and

apartment properties often age slowly and gracefully. Look around your own neighborhood. Look at the apartments that have been there for thirty or forty years, the business establishments that have stood in place for twenty or thirty. Many—possibly most—will be in first-rate condition, performing in thriving fashion, ready for another twenty or thirty years of service.

In the quest for business property, be curious. If you see something you like, and which you think might be within your means, ask one of the tenants whose property it is. Sometimes you will get surprising and helpful information.

Recently I stopped in at my favorite service station, a major oil company facility which forms an attractive portion of a small business cluster near my home. In addition to the station, which does a thriving business and will no doubt continue to do so in this well-established neighborhood, a convenience store and garden shop are also on the property. I had visited the place for years, but never inquired about its ownership. In this instance, I asked the station operator about its owners.

"Oh, it belongs to John Smith's wife and her sister," he promptly replied, "and John told me the other day the girls need to sell it. I'd like to buy it myself," he continued, "but it's just a little rich for me."

I knew John Smith and contacted him later in the day, receiving confirmation of the operator's story. Within a week, our group had contracted to buy the property. In this case, the owners were fortunately not interested in heavy front cash and so we arranged the transaction on the basis of a small down payment and a fifteen-year payout (with regular monthly payments of principal and interest), giving as security a first mortgage on the land. We pay the rents into a trust which the owners have established for their children. There was no real estate brokerage involved, of course, and our down payment was only 10 percent. The rents will more than pay the mortgage, taxes, insurance, and predictable maintenance charges and even leave a little from which we can recapture the 10 percent.

It never hurts, and rarely costs, to make inquiries.

Don't be overly ambitious as you take your first steps into the field of real estate investment. Look for a 30,000-square-foot shopping facility instead of a 100,000-foot operation. Look for a 24-unit apartment instead of a 200-unit complex. One thing will inevitably lead to another, and there will be ample time to go for the bigger items after you've had some actual experience with smaller ones. Quite apart from receiving some basic education in the field of real estate, you will also be able to make early judgments on the compatibility of your investment group.

Remember, as we noted earlier, in almost any real estate transaction you will be talking about lots of dollars. For example, that 30,000-foot mini-center or twenty-four-unit apartment will, in either instance and under the most modest of projections, be spinning out $60,000 a year (at rentals of $2 a square foot on the former and $200 per month per unit on the latter). Thus, even when you start small, you'll be acquiring what by the standards in any other field of investment would be a rather large holding.

Zoning and Restrictive Covenants

Zoning has been accomplished throughout most of the United States and in almost every city. At the threshold of any transaction you will need to make inquiry as to (a) whether the property in which you are interested is zoned at all and (b) if it is, in what classification and with what permitted uses.

There are many types of property you can acquire

and much you can do with land after you've bought it. Residentially, the range is from single-family use to high-rise apartment. Commercially, the choices are even broader, ranging from an office in a quiet residential neighborhood on the one extreme, to a manufacturing plant on the other. You may, of course, build any kind of structure you like on land that you own, provided you are within zoning—and, of course, building-code—limitations.

Here again, incidentally, you will want to be conversant with the zoning ordinances of your city or of the community in which your property is located. Such ordinances are normally available in booklet form at the local planning office for a nominal charge. Check particularly to see whether the applicable zoning law is pyramidal (permitting the construction of any type of building which involves a less restrictive use than the zoning classification indicates, e.g., residential buildings permitted in an industrially zoned area) or exclusive, i.e., permitting only such uses as are specified in the ordinance or a given zoning category (e.g., only a manufacturing or processing operation in an industrial zone). Obviously, if it's pyramidal you have a great deal more latitude.

One should probably not generalize about land values as related to zoning categories, but I will do so anyway. As a rule, land zoned for retail uses is worth more than land zoned for other commercial endeavors, including manufacturing. Multi-family land is less valuable than business and industrial property but up the scale from land zoned exclusively for single-family residential use. All of the foregoing have a higher valuation than farmland. In descending order of valuation, then, you would generally go from retail to industrial to multi-family residential to single-family residential.

Cautionary note: Always check the zoning classification. Don't rely on what the seller tells you. Frequently his "I'm sure it's zoned for business" means "I really don't know, but it *ought* to be zoned that way."

Of course, zoning for a given tract can be, and frequently is, changed, but this is a decision for local governing bodies and often becomes political, subject more to the pressures of forces for or against a particular rezoning effort than to good zoning practices. Thus, again generally speaking, it is best to buy land which doesn't present any zoning problem, immediate or foreseeable. If someone wants to buy your property but only if it is rezoned to another classification, and the proposal is otherwise palatable, condition your sales agreement on *buyer's* getting the zoning change approved rather than putting that burden on yourself.

One other comment about zoning may be in order. Occasionally a property use does not conform to the comprehensive zoning plan. You might, for example, have an opportunity to purchase a convenience store in a heavily residential area and learn on checking the zoning map at your local planning office that the site is zoned for residential use only. This ambiguity will have resulted from the fact that the building you are studying was there before the most recent zoning of the area and that the planners felt it was long-range residential territory. For constitutional reasons, among others, existing uses in such cases are permitted to continue and may in some instances (again, the ordinance will tell you which ones) be enlarged, rebuilt if destroyed by fire, and so on.

To repeat: *Always* determine the zoning classification for any property you are interested in. If it's zoned for business, what kinds of uses are permitted? Most ordinances will list these generically (e.g., stores, movie theaters, garden shops in Business-1). If it's not zoned for business but has an existing business use protected because it predated the passage of the zoning ordinance, what are the limitations imposed upon an owner? What addition, if any, is permitted to the existing structure? What use can be made of the property if the building is destroyed by fire or other casualty? Of course, if it *is* a preexisting, or so-called nonconforming use, then its value to you is less than would otherwise be the case, and this would be a negotiating factor, obviously operating in your favor.

Yet another form of restriction on land use is imposed by restrictive covenants. These are conditions imposed by deed and in most, but not all, instances will relate to preserving the use of land for single-family residential purposes. If your house is located in a residential subdivision, chances are the property is encumbered with restrictive covenants. These are generally enforceable and can only be waived by the signatures of all owners in the affected area. Restrictive covenants will override zoning restrictions. For example, if the city zoning ordinance establishes apartment usage as appropriate for a given section of the community, and much of that area is burdened with single-family-use covenants, no apartments may be built on property thus restricted, notwithstanding the more liberal permissiveness of the ordinance.

Don't Build—Don't Operate

In this book, written for the weekend real estate investor, and with one exception, I am suggesting strongly that, at least initially, you stay away from construction—that you buy either empty land (with a view to holding it for appreciation) or existing apartments, office buildings, or retail centers. In succeeding chapters I will explain my reasons for this and provide you with suggestions designed to help you in making acquisitions of any of these.

For the moment, I will simply support this recommendation by emphasizing that when you buy existing buildings, or raw land, you are dealing with known quantities—known costs, known incomes. In the case of income property, you are also sparing yourself the time and headaches which are inevitably involved when you build your own.

Another key imperative for the amateur is to stay passive. "Passive" in this sense means not getting involved in the operation of any business that is on your property. It means owning property and renting it and letting it go at that. It means not getting into the land-development business, not getting into resort property, not—in a phrase—spending your amateur energies in a professional's ballpark.

Don't be a swinger. Some years ago, before we had embarked on our real estate investment venture, one of my friends became fascinated with the idea of investing in resort property. He had been hypnotized by a sales pitch delivered on behalf of a new North Carolina coastal development in which the pitchman, aided by the omnipresent slide presentation, had dramatized the growth potential of investment in recreational property. Using bar charts, the salesman had demonstrated that over the preceding ten years no investment category had been as growth oriented as real estate and that among real estate investments, none had grown in value as rapidly as those in resort properties.

My colleague was persuasive—so persuasive that several of us optioned and later bought some western North Carolina mountain property, thinking to strengthen our humble resources substantially. At that time, banks too were enchanted with resort properties, and we had no trouble obtaining a large development loan from a local lender.

Then we (or, more accurately, contractors under our direction) sprang to the development task, under a master plan which looked very workable on a flat piece of paper but became nearly impossible to achieve when translated into the grading and earth-moving problems presented by an aging western North Carolina mountain. As the dogwood bloomed, the problems blossomed. As the winds of winter blew, they multiplied. The contractor had failed to consider that vast rock deposits lay just beneath the surface of the golf course site (by my own estimate, approximately 90 percent of all the rock in the Blue Ridge Mountains was contained within this otherwise innocent-looking 100-acre tract).

It was impossible to get the water in and the sewerage out. On top of all that, the planner misjudged the skill level of southern skiers, designing the ski slopes for experts rather than for the beginners who, we later and painfully learned, would constitute the bulk of market demand.

When the property was finally operational, management and sales problems occupied an altogether disproportionate amount of our time. Instead of the simple three- or four-person partnership I'll be recommending to you shortly, we had put together an assembly of ten businessmen, none of whom knew the slightest thing about building or operating a recreational property. As costs soared and income lagged, frictions developed among individuals who had joined together in a spirit of friendship.

We sold, of course. To professionals. At a loss.

The moral to us was clear and expensive, but I pass it on to you postpaid and duty-free. Let the pros do the dirty work. You just mow the lawn.

Options and Sales Agreements

Most real estate transactions are officially commenced by seller's giving buyer an option to purchase the former's property. An option may extend for any period agreed on between the parties but must be supported by a quid pro quo, i.e., something given by the buyer to the seller. Usually the QPQ takes the form of a little money (it can be as small as a dollar or as large as the parties want to make it; normally the amount of earnest money will vary directly with the length of the option). Most option agreements provide that seller's payment will be credited against the purchase price if the option is in fact exercised and forfeited if it is not (unless seller is unable to deliver a marketable title, in which case it will be returned to buyer).

No agreement respecting the sale of real estate is enforceable unless it is evidenced by a written memorandum, signed by the owner or other individual or entity with authority to sell. This proposition has been true since the time of Charles II and is codified in almost every state under what are called statutes of frauds (after their progenitor statute, titled "An Act for the Prevention of Frauds and Perjuries").

Typically, such laws read like the North Carolina enactment:

All contracts to sell or convey any lands . . . or any interest in or concerning them . . . shall be void unless said contract, or some memorandum or note thereof, be put in writing and signed by the party to be charged therewith, or by some other person by him thereto lawfully authorized.*

No great formality is required to make such a memorandum legally binding. "In consideration of $100 paid by him to me this day, January 1, 1978, I

*General Statutes of North Carolina, 22-2.

hereby give an option to buy my twelve-unit apartment at West and Sunset Streets to Joe Buyer for $100,000 and give him sixty days to close the deal. If the title is not good, I'll give him his money back. (signed) Joe Seller." Joe Seller is on the hook.

Because of the uniqueness of land, agreements for its sale can be specifically enforced against the seller, but not against the buyer, where a contract of sale (as opposed to a simple option) is involved. This is an extremely important element in real estate investment. With certain minor exceptions, if you contract to buy some other form of property and seller refuses to comply with his part of the bargain, you may sue him for damages but you cannot compel him to deliver the goods. In the case of land, you may ask the court to order performance under the agreement, and if the document is legally binding, the court will accommodate you.

In the absence of some recorded agreement to the contrary, and in most states, all buildings become part of the land on which they are constructed. What you see is what you will get if you buy the property.

Sometimes, instead of acquiring title to the land itself, you may find it convenient, or only possible, to acquire a leasehold interest for a long term of years. In a few states (e.g., New York and Maryland) a multitude of property is handled on this basis. In this book, we are going to look at leasing of land in the broadest way, since techniques and usages will sometimes vary markedly from state to state. Your attorney will be able to advise you about this.

An option to buy is to be distinguished from a contract to buy (or, as it is popularly and more accurately designated, a contract of sale). In the former, you can walk away from the transaction if, within the option period, you decide that the property is simply not for you, or even if it is, that the financing is beyond your reach. All you lose is your time and earnest money. A contract of sale, on the other hand, commits both buyer and seller.

Just as price is the figure buyer and seller agree on, so other terms may be as flexible as the parties like. Front money, time for closing, amortization period, mortgage provisions—with respect to any and all of these, the buyer and seller may do as they please. Your stockbroker will find this hard to believe, but that's the way it is.

Two
Your Organization

Two heads are better than one, three skills are more than two, group endeavors are more apt to succeed than individual ones. None of the foregoing is always true, but generally speaking, more is better. In advising about real estate investing I take the view that you will be better off if you form a small group of fellow investors and make it a common enterprise. If you follow this approach and go beyond four, your group will tend to become unwieldy.

Land can be owned in a myriad of ways. You can form a corporation and take title in the corporate name. You can simply put title in all your names individually, in which case the law will impose the status of what is called a tenancy in common on your joint ownership.

(Each member owns an undivided interest in the whole.) You can create a trust, letting one individual hold the legal title for the benefit of all of you. Or you can form a partnership.

One by one, let's briefly examine these alternatives.

Corporation

Incorporation? Forget it. If your property sustains losses, you want to be able to offset your share of these against ordinary income. Obviously, you can't do this if your corporation holds a title. *It* takes the losses. If it makes money (through the sale of property or otherwise), it will pay a corporate tax, thus diminishing the amount available to you, and on what is left—if, as stockholders, you pay it over to yourselves—you will pay a further tax.

If you try to get property out of the corporation in order to place it in your individual names or in a partnership, you will be confronted with a tax on any gain in value of the property since the corporation acquired it, even though all you are doing is shifting it from one form of ownership to another (in the eyes of the IRS you are shifting it from one *owner*—the corporation—to another—the partnership). There is a way around this in situations where a tract of raw land is the only corporate asset, but it is fairly involved and almost certain to invite scrutiny.

Of course, all expenses, as well as depreciation taken, are charged to the corporation. Thus, and in most instances, you derive no direct tax shelter.

Federal tax laws do permit certain corporations—referred to by the section of the Internal Revenue Code which provides for this anomaly, subchapter S corporations—to be taxed, in many but not all respects, like partnerships. To qualify as a subchapter S company, yours must have no more than ten stockholders (no problems there) and be involved in active (as opposed to passive) corporate enterprise. Simple corporate land-holding, or simple ownership of rent-producing properties, in other words, will not buy you a sub S ticket. If more than 20 percent of the company revenue comes from rental income (and unless significant services are rendered the renter), you are passive through and through.

Tenancy in Common

A tenancy in common is or can be cumbersome. All deeds or other instruments affecting your property must be signed by the individual tenants and their spouses. Explanations have to be made in such instances and, on occasion, disagreements between couples can slow progress materially—maybe fatally.

You can simplify the signature problem by giving a power of attorney—signed by owners and spouses—to one or more of your group, but other procedural problems would remain. How broad should the power be? For how long should it be granted? Which and how many of you should hold it? How would you ensure that individual tax returns would coincide as to transactions affecting all of you? Obviously these questions can be answered in ways amenable to the power-of-attorney format, but they do suggest that tenancies in common are not the simplest form of ownership for investors.

In any case, the tenancy-in-common form solves no problems of common ownership. By whatever means, you must provide for control, the demise of an owner, financing, and disposition of sales proceeds.

Trust

Trust agreements are not in popular use for landowning purposes of the kind we are describing. One of you would have to serve as trustee under an instrument providing this officer (or officers—you could have cotrustees) with specific powers. All transactions would be in the name of the trustee or trustees. As an ownership vehicle it would provide direct personal benefits (the trust itself would not be taxable) and in that regard, at least, would stand on the same footing as tenancy in common or partnership. It has some awkward aspects, not least of which would be delineating the framework of trustee authority, and for this, among other reasons, is not customarily used as a simple landowning agency.

Partnership

A simple partnership offers the best of all worlds. Individual benefits stemming from depreciation and interest payments are available to each partner in the same manner as though he owned the property individually (though, of course, limited to his fractional interest in the partnership). One partner or two (or whatever number is agreed on in the partnership contract) can sign for and bind the partnership. With ease, separate properties may be placed in separate ventures, permitting flexibility in ownership. A trading name may be used (e.g., Queensland Shopping Center) for business purposes. Separate tax returns are required for each partnership, of course, but the partnership itself pays no income tax. (Taxes, if any, flow through to the partners. Your tax-return preparer simply sends to each partner a form which the partner attaches to his own 1040, reflecting profits or losses the partnership has sustained.) Remember that with real estate you may show a loss (which can be offset against ordinary income from other sources) while at the same time enjoying a positive cash flow.

You have read of, and perhaps invested in, a so-called *syndicate of partners*. These are generally *limited partnerships*, the limited partners having the benefits of flow-through deductions for interest and depreciation, and other expenses, but not being bound by the obligations of partnership. A limited partner, for example, has no liability for debts incurred by the partnership and may not under any circumstances (and without the unanimous consent of all the limited partners) be subjected to further assessment. On the other hand, neither does the limited partner have any say in management of the group's affairs. Operation is under the sole control of a general partner or partners.

Limited partnerships, especially the larger ones, have come under close scrutiny by state and federal regulatory authorities in recent years. Their organizers, to keep the structure within the protective confines of a partnership, walk a very narrow line. If they overstep it, the IRS might determine that the group is in fact— and in law—a corporation and impose the tax levy accordingly, depriving limited partners of the shelter which they had thought was theirs.

Anyway, limited partnerships are generally formed to take on the heavy projects—the $15-million office building or the $5-million shopping center. You are in another classification. You are a weekend investor who, with two or three friends, wants to speculate modestly in real estate. For you and your group the so-called general partnership is the best vehicle.

In Appendix 1 you will find a simple partnership

form which, with minor variations for each project, we have found adequate. In most jurisdictions, there is no requirement that this document be recorded in the public registry (or register of deeds office), but it *is* necessary to record a certificate reflecting the partnership name and the identities and addresses of the partners.

It is important to make provision for the survival of the organization in the event of a partner's death, due to the fact that the partnership would terminate in the absence of such provision.

In-house management rules—such as signatory requirements for checks and other documents—can also be established by the agreement itself. With a corporation, your charter is the creating and enabling document. Bylaws are separately imposed on that. With a partnership, the agreement is everything.

Except in those cases where the stockholders have personally endorsed a corporate obligation, creditors may not go beyond corporate assets and get at the shareholders individually. This is not true with a general partnership. Partners are individually responsible for debts of the unit, and thus their personal assets are on the line. It is well to be always mindful of this, but if you proceed in accordance with the general investing standards suggested in succeeding chapters, you will have little or no real personal exposure.

Group Formation

Do not limit yourself to a narrow circle of friends. Make up your trio or quartet from people you encounter in business or know through a civic club. Pick people who are compatible and trustworthy.

There is nothing magic or sacred in composing such a group, although legal, accounting, and real estate skills are nice to have aboard. Butchers, bakers, candlestick makers; plumbers, preachers, grammar school teachers; any vocation can play. Over the years we've assembled a list of ten individuals, each known to and, so far as I can tell, liked by the others, and from this number we can almost always arouse a sufficient amount of interest to take advantage of good opportunities. With ten people on the occasional prowl, opportunities tend to turn up. We have a lawyer, two subcontractors, one general contractor, a merchant, a salesman, an electrical engineer, an architect, a dentist, and a real estate broker.

The four of us who started the project still own most of our partnerships, but when necessary we summon one or two of the other six, or one of them contacts one of us. It has worked beautifully.

I do not suggest that you should do the same, but in our groups none of us charges professional fees for services unless some specific, extraordinary labor is involved. For example, the wife of one of our members is an accountant and she keeps the books of our modest multi-family residential holdings, for a modest charge. My secretary handles other interim bookkeeping, and we use an accounting firm for quarterly updates and preparation of tax returns. If our legal work becomes unusually burdensome in connection with acquisition of a given project, we tax the group for that. If we need some work done on a building, the contractor handles the chore and of course is paid.

We have no property managers as such (except in the case of one shopping center where we retained the manager who had looked after the development from its inception), no partner fees as such, and we never divide up cash accumulations.

What if a partner wants out? We've had it happen only once. The remaining partners bought his interest, and he emerged with a tidy, if not dramatic, profit. It is well, however, to anticipate that the problem may arise, and you can provide for a means of valuing the interest of the departing member in your partnership agreement (to be employed if the issue cannot be resolved by agreement). Arbitration is the usual answer to a valuation impasse, with the remaining partners to choose one appraiser, the outgoing partner to choose another, and these two to select an umpire. The unpredictables—sickness, loss of employment, transfer—are unavoidable, but try to limit the chances that they will affect your group by careful initial selection. Assemble people who are stable in the community and blessed with steady incomes. Be wary of big-spender types. Those who regularly flirt with insolvency often tend to marry it. In the event of one partner's death, his interest can be handled in much the same way as if he had voluntarily retired.

Naturally, if we sell the holdings of a particular partnership, we dissolve the venture and divide at least enough to cover the capital gains tax we will each have to pay (assuming, as has always been the case up to now—with the exception of the resort debacle—that the sale was profitable).

Among other things, the foregoing tells you that none of our investors has a problem living off his earned income, and this salubrious condition is an absolutely essential prerequisite to setting up the kind of program outlined in this book.

In brief, then, do not launch a real estate investment plan to provide extra income for yourself. Make a commitment to equity growth. The income will later—and abundantly.

Of course, an element of risk is inherent i

worthwhile investment. There is no way to avoid it. Thus, if riskless venture is the only game you want to play, real estate is not for you. Not much else is, either.

Record Keeping

Someone needs to keep the records. With respect to income property and the receipts and outgo it generates, the job is obviously more time-consuming (and of course involves considerably more responsibility) than is the case with nonproductive raw land. My experience has been that in almost any group you can assemble, one of its members will have a special talent and liking for this part of the job. Or a member will have in his own business organization a bookkeeper whose services will be available on the basis of a modest fee arrangement.

We have never had the slightest problem with this aspect of our partnerships. I mention it simply to remind you of this rather obvious need.

Accountants and Lawyers

Of course, your accountant will prepare the annual partnership returns and will be available for interim consultation and advice. Do certain proposed expenditures qualify as capital (in which case they would qualify for long-term depreciation), or is it a maintenance item (in which even you would write it off in the year of expenditure)? Interest is deductible when paid. How about that point or two (1- to 2-percent premium paid a lender at the time a loan is consummated) disbursed to Pacific Mortgage Company when you bought the apartments? (This has to be spread over the life of the loan.) Questions like this will arise regularly. Your accountant, or lawyer, will be pleased to answer them for you. Once you've settled in with your choice of each of these professionals, you will find it easy, and remarkably inexpensive—often cost-free, in fact—to check with them frequently.

If your initial group does not number among its members an accountant or a lawyer, seek out one of each of these professional breeds early on. One of you will surely have had dealings, individually or through his company, with an accountant. If his experience has been good, maybe that's the person you want. If it hasn't, or if for any reason none of you has a preference for his accountant, ask around. The same holds true with respect to your choice of counsel.

My advice would be that for the size and types of investments we are discussing, you'll be best served by an accountant practicing in a small firm. What is "small" will depend on the size of your community. A small law firm has similar advantages and will (unless the firm is exclusively concerned with trial work—a relatively rare occurrence) have at least one person who works solely in real estate. People working with you in such offices will tend to take a more personal interest in your enterprises. They will also—as a rule—be more accessible than their peers who labor in the giant-sized firms.

You will—and should—tend to stick with your original choices of accountant and lawyer, so make them carefully.

Banking

I will speak about this in more detail later but for now will only assert the need of a short-term, front-money financing source. This will usually be a bank and, more particularly—since banks, like all human agencies, operate through individuals—a sympathetic bank official. If you are on terms with more than one banker, in more than one bank, you are just that much better off.

Bank loan officers, especially those with some experience, are invaluable in many ways. First, they are among the few people who can, with authority, utter such musical phrases as "Why, of course, we'd love to let you have the money." Almost—but not quite—as important, their advice is free and, unlike the usual worth of this gratuitous commodity, often quite valuable. Good loan officers can almost sense whether a given project has merit. They will review more investment proposals in a year than you will be concerned with in ten—or twenty. So, even if they say no, and offer this negative judgment on the basis of the proposal itself rather than your personal credit ratings, they may have helped you more than you will ever know—or would care to know.

As with other mercantile establishments, so with banks: They don't all have the good buys at the same time. You will need to impose on the various banking loyalties of all your group's members, but in time you will probably find that one or two of these lenders will tend to become special favorites.

For the moment, I will simply lay this one further observation on the table. Banks, which earn a substantial portion of their profits from lending money and charging for it, would rather say yes than no to your request for help.

Three
How to Find the Property and What to Do When You Find It

Perhaps the single most difficult aspect of real estate investment is finding the property. Your local newspaper will be filled with advertisements of real estate that is for sale. Any broker* you call will be able to list bargains galore for you. An hour's drive along any

*The definition of broker employed by the North Carolina Real Estate Licensing Board is typical: "A real estate broker . . . is any person, partnership, association or corporation, who [sic] for a compensation or valuable consideration or promise thereof lists or offers to list, sells or offers to sell, buys or offers to buy, auctions or offers to auction (specifically not including a mere crier of sales), or negotiates the purchase or sale or exchange of real estate, or who sells or offers to sell leases of whatever character, or rents or offers to rent any real estate or the improvement thereon, for others."

roadway will yield a rich harvest of "For Sale" signs. Working for you at all times will be the general proposition that everything is for sale at some price. As with any economic rule of thumb, this one has its exceptions—a treasured objet d'art, the collection of letters from an ancestor—but, by and large, and whatever it is, depend on it, it is for sale. A second proposition is that the best buys are often to be found in those properties whose owners, until approached, may never have really thought of selling. Still, it is difficult to find the precise kind of property you might want at a given time. One simply has to invoke the ancient biblical admonition, "Seek and ye shall find."

How Best to Seek?

The Broker   Do not discount the help that a good broker can provide. Ideally—but by no means necessarily—you would have such an individual in your group. On the other hand, do not undervalue your own abilities. Real estate commissions will run anywhere from 5 to 10 percent, in some instances more, and this figure, whatever it amounts to, must come out of the purchase price. You will pay it or the seller will pay it, but it will be paid, almost always at the front.

At the outset, then, we must recognize that if it can be avoided, you have saved that much. If you are buying a $100,000 tract of unimproved land (commissions generally run highest for this type of property), you can save approximately $10,000 if you can accomplish it without the intervening use of a broker. However, if the property *has* been listed with a broker for sale, the commission *must* be paid, whether you heard of the land's availability through this agent or not. *Always* ask a seller if the property has been or is now listed. If he tells you it has been but isn't now, ask him when the listing expired (sometimes listing contracts provide for a carry-over of thirty days—or comparable time period—for commission purposes). A broker can be extremely helpful in negotiations, but remember that his commission will normally vary directly with the purchase price.

It could happen that a broker will approach you about an attractive property with which you are acquainted and which he has reason to believe might be available, although it is not officially listed with him. You could, of course, express your appreciation and make your own investigation. However, the better course of action would be to discuss with the agent the question of assisting you and settling on a fee, contingent on ultimate purchase by you. Even if you do not ultimately acquire the property, the agent will recall your fairness, and one fine day he might bring you the most desirable deal you'd ever want to see.

Advertising   A large portion of real estate sales are made by sellers who never listed their property, never advertised it, in many instances never really planned to sell it. Someone has approached them directly and simply asked whether they would sell, and if so, for how much. Perhaps they responded to a newspaper advertisement appearing in the "Property Wanted" section of their local daily: "Wanted: large acreage tract on west side of center city. Please write, giving details, c/o Box 49." Or "Wanted—small shopping facility or convenience store. Please write, giving particulars, c/o Box 50."

Both the direct approach and the invitational ad are often productive. As to the former, identifying ownership of a property which appeals to you is easy. Every piece of land in your county carries an identifying lot and block number at the local tax office. You simply locate the property on the tax assessor's map and an office clerk will tell you how to proceed from there. Customarily this is an easy, cost-free route to knowledge. In addition to giving you ownership data, the tax maps will give you, often with precise accuracy, physical dimensions and, of course, valuations (which may or may not equate with market value) for land and improvements. You will even find plot plans, outlining the improvements on the property, showing exterior dimensions and interior amenities. In most counties, copies of maps showing the property you are interested in are available on request to anyone who asks and proffers the proper tariff (in our county, 50¢ per copy).

Local Opportunities As a rule, it is better to play in your own ballpark. Stick with the territory you know. You—or some of you—will hear about the things that are going on in your community. You will read of proposed zoning changes. You will see with your own eyes where most of the building activity is. Every community has its directional indicators. Business is moving east or south. The best apartments are rising in the west. Most rehabilitation of older buildings is taking place on the north side of center city. You will be seeing and reading of this regularly. As you become more interested in land development, you will be more sensitive to what is happening around you. Through the local press, you will learn of proposed tax increases or road widenings and major construction projects. All of this information will help you make educated judgments concerning property that otherwise interests you.

None of the foregoing is to say that you shouldn't venture into an adjoining county. You will find, as you get into your program, that you will hear of available real estate in many locations, from many sources. If one of your group comes upon something that looks extremely inviting, don't reject it out of hand simply because it is in another town, but don't buy it until you have educated yourself thoroughly concerning the tract and its environs. Most chambers of commerce will have good, reasonably objective information, and in each case you will want to check with the local planning board office, which normally will have the most reliable news available concerning community land use, current and projected.

But, I repeat: Unless the other town's grass is a whole lot greener, stay local.

Downtown   The demise of downtown is being bemoaned almost everywhere these days, and not without some reason. Massive shopping malls and older, conventionally designed shopping centers have lured the shopper toward suburbia. Center-city stores which had stood for years like monuments have moved the way of all the flesh, so that now in villages large and small, empty midtown storefronts punctuate every block.

Already and all over we are seeing signs of downtown property renewal. Taxpayers are balking at the unending expense of extending utility lines further into the countryside, building the roads that must take the dwellers out there, and paying for the police and fire and school services suburbia requires.

Rents for new construction exceed by wide margins those charged by downtown owners, and the difference is quite simply explained in terms of supply and demand—*and* by the age of the interior properties. Never again will construction costs be as low as when these old buildings were erected.

Many downtown buildings are owned by bank trust departments which have looked after the estates of the original owners for years. Most such landlords are taking whatever rent they can get, and many of them will sell their properties to anyone who will make an offer. It doesn't even have to be reasonable, but it probably shouldn't be absurd. Somewhere in between.

Older houses on the fringes of center city have suddenly become a hot item in the real estate marketplace, particularly among younger people. These properties are being bought and refurbished. History has always repeated itself, and, at least in the matter of urban-core revival, we are seeing the validity of this time-honored proposition reasserted.

Notwithstanding the great land exodus to suburbia—and exurbia—over the last two decades, a central fact of social proclivity remains unchanged. By and large, people like to be around other people. Athens in 450 B.C. had a population of 200,000, and all of these folks lived and moved and had their being in an area 2 miles square. In fifteen minutes of leisurely ambulation, one could walk from the edge of the city to its center. Florence in the fifteenth century was similarly sized physically and contained 70,000 people.

As the energy crisis mounts, as costs of public services soar, as history repeats itself, downtown store buildings, like aging but close-in residences, are going to look more and more attractive. The people of Athens and Florence might have been right after all. Be prepared for this.

Look around your city. Observe the many institutions, public and private, whose headquarters are located in the city's center. Courthouses, banks, large office buildings, a few tenaciously loyal department stores—these are, and in most cases will remain, there. People (consumers) are in these buildings, and they will remain there too, at least for five days of every week.

Pick a sector of your downtown which—after careful study—you feel is strongly viable, and within this area take a look at vacant properties. Don't be dissuaded by the appearance of a building whose location you especially like. Let one of your friends who is interested in design have a look at its facade. Some imagination, some awnings, some paint can work wonders on the front of an ancient building and give the whole structure a brand-new and distinctive look. Remember that with downtown property you don't have to worry about what the sides or back look like and there is no landscaping problem.

If everything fits, and the price and financing are palatable, you could do worse than to option it and start shopping for a tenant. Let a good real estate agent be your tenant shopper.

Many of these old buildings have second and third floors, but few of them have elevators. Real estate appraisers will tell you that such space is valueless. Well, maybe it is and maybe it isn't. Restaurateurs in some of our largest cities have done very well with walk-up second-floor facilities, especially if the street side is fully glassed or windowed. It is space in any event, and as space—and particularly center-city space—becomes costlier of acquisition, it will—no matter its difficulty of access—become more valuable.

In most communities, the chamber of commerce, the newspaper, the merchants' association, and other equally patriotic agencies are anxious to keep the downtown areas healthy. Owners and tenants alike will be boosted in their efforts to assist in this ongoing project.

One of my longtime clients operates a discount jewelry store in our center city. He does a land-office business. Recently I asked him if there was a special secret to his success.

"Well, I advertise a lot," he said. "I learned early that advertising expense is deductible. But more than that I think people still like to shop downtown, particularly if the stores offer the merchandise. There's a variety of shopping experiences available here that you can't get in any mall or shopping center, and everything seems a little more personal. Apart from that," he added, "my rent is one-seventh what it would be in the new mall!"

We are going to be seeing more and more of this breed of businessperson, and so I'm suggesting you might want to help one find a good home.

As mentioned, many if not most downtown properties have been long owned by one family and title is frequently in a bank trustee which administers the property under the terms of a trust instrument. What a trustee can and cannot do with such holdings depends upon the language of the trust-creating document. Usually it will give an express power of sale to the trustee, but it does not always or even often authorize expressly or by implication a sale with long-term financing by seller.

Let's assume that you have found a property you like, that it is owned by a trust, that the trustee does want to sell it, that the building is sound and the price right, but that the sale has to be for cash. If the property has been in trust for a long time and not advertised for sale, you should be in a position to negotiate a lengthy option. Get one as long as you can because, most probably, we are talking about an empty building.

If the trustee is, as will likely be the case, a bank, make inquiry as to whether that institution's commercial loan department might be interested in making a short-term loan. By hypothesis, the property will be in need of some repair, and of course you will be jazzing up its face side extensively. You need the short-term loan to cover the situation while you are making some preliminary studies (and finding a tenant) and pending the time when—building redone and tenant signed—you'll be seeking permanent financing.

Use the option period for all of these purposes, but make the search for permanent financing your priority quest. Assure the proposed permanent lender that you will be making extensive improvements on the property; if possible, have some drawings done which will graphically reflect the changes you will make to the front of the building.

Many downtown properties have required revaluation for tax purposes because rents have dropped dramatically over the past few years. Ascertain from the tax assessor's office (and this before you obtain your option) the tax history on this property. If the tax is disproportionately high, make its reduction a condition of purchase and put the burden on the trustee to seek and obtain the revaluation.

Don't under any circumstances invest a heavy option payment in a venture like this *unless* you have a strong tenant already committed to you. In the absence of such a commitment, your option is money invested in a purely speculative enterprise and should be kept to an absolute minimum.

Sell the trustee on this by pointing out that you are getting into the project as a public service, doing your bit for the salvation and salvage of the CBD (code name for central business district).

Bargain Basement   All of us are familiar with the so-called courthouse-door sale. Property in an estate is being sold to pay debts of the decedent. Land is being sold so that money can be divided among heirs or other owners (called partition proceedings, such sales are necessitated by failure of the owners to agree on an equitable division or because the land is inherently not susceptible to division). Mortgages are being foreclosed. Tax liens are being asserted, or the property of bankrupts or judgment debtors are being sold.

Many such sales receive no more advertising than that provided through the fine-print, stodgily worded legal notices appearing in your local journal's classified section. Sometimes such advertisements will contain a tax-map reference (remember our earlier comment on tracking these down) or other identifying comment. More often they will simply give what is called a metes and bounds description, that is, dimensions and boundary directions of the tract without other definite aid. In these cases, you can, if you are interested, get further aid by calling the commissioner or lawyer who signs the ad.

If someone in your group has time to track these notices, you might find that they will lead you to an occasional bonanza. Forced sales of this sort are usually handled within the following framework: They are at auction. The high bidder must leave with the selling official a deposit (usually 5 percent) at the time of sale. For a specified period (usually ten days), such sales are subject to upset (meaning that one may, by making a minimum addition to the bid price, compel another public sale). This procedure continues until there are no further upset bids and the high existing offer is approved (or—as is sometimes the case—rejected) by the court.

There are no title warranties. The court-appointed seller is simply a conduit. Usually a lawyer will be present at such sales and will often know, at least in a general way, something about the property's legal status. Of course, you can have the title searched (though not certified) before you bid. If the land appeals to you, money spent with a title lawyer for this advance information would be a prudent expenditure.

Naturally, all such sales are for cash to the finally confirmed bidder, so you would need to have financing assurance ahead of your entry into this sort of sales proceeding.

While it is important not to suppress bids (urge people to stay away from the sale), it is perfectly all right to sell a high bid, and indeed this happens frequently.

In general, you will find that the best buys at forced sales of this kind are on unimproved land.

What to Do When You Find

Preliminary Evaluation   Once you have acquired information about a particular piece of property, either naked land or income-producing business or multi-family residential, decide what you are willing to pay for it. (Remember that you can hedge your bets by obtaining an option and the option can contain as many conditions as you and the seller may agree on, as, for example, the condition of being able to obtain adequate financing or a permanent loan in a minimum amount.) If your study of the property tells you it is a good buy at $100,000, then be prepared to pay that amount and no more. Naturally, you can try to induce the seller to part with it for less. Normally—as to income property—the owner will provide you with operational figures. If for any reason these are difficult to come by, ask questions of others. Tenants, for example: "Hi. Just curious. We're looking at some property like this. Just wondering what kind of rent you pay here?"

Of course, property taxes are a matter of record, and insurance and maintenance costs are subject to an educated speculation.

I emphasize the importance of making this preliminary judgment of value. Many otherwise excellent situations are missed because buyers prefer haggling to buying. If you can buy at the numbers you like, and you want the land, then make every effort to tie it up. We recently lost the best purchase opportunity I have ever encountered (a shopping center) because one of our group of four was convinced that the owner would reduce his price, and the rest of us let him carry the day. In fact, the owner subsequently raised his price and sold to an out-of-state venturer. Like time and tide, good real estate purchase possibilities wait for no man—or partnership.

Option An option agreement gives you, for the time and price set out, an exclusive right to purchase the specified property. An option, if executed with the requisite formality (meaning, in essence, with the signature of seller, acknowledged before and certified to by a notary public or other authorized official), may be recorded in the public registry; when and if it is, it becomes notice to the world that you and you alone control the disposition of the affected land for the option period.

This is a protective measure for you, but there may well be situations in which either you or the seller does not want the world to be apprised that the transaction is being considered. In such a case, if you trust the seller to honor the option, you can dispense with the formality of registering it. Let your judgment be your guide. Appendix 2 is a sample of an option agreement, but options are highly malleable critters and the parties can load them with a variety of conditions.

Naturally, option agreements will provide that the property be *owned by optioner;* that the title be *unencumbered* except as to any burdens referred to in the agreement; and, if it is income producing, that leases, expenses, and rents are as represented by optioner.

We recently optioned an apartment project via an agreement providing, among other things, that "we be able to obtain satisfactory financing." Satisfactory to whom? It didn't say, but naturally, it meant us. How much is enough to be satisfactory to us? It didn't say, but naturally, it meant as much as we needed to make the purchase economically viable. As it developed, we were able to get "satisfactory financing." If we hadn't been, then our good-faith deposit would have been returned. It is only retained by the optioner when failure to purchase results from a decision or fault on the part of the optionee.

Unless the agreement provides otherwise, you can sell the option. It often happens. Sometimes (you should always try for this) the option provides for renewal at buyer's—optionee's—election and on payment of additional earnest money. If you can get more than one renewal, splendid. By all means, do so. "This option, subject to all its terms and conditions, may be renewed for an additional sixty days by giving at least fifteen days' notice to optioner mailed to the address given below and payment of an additional $500." The agreement will provide that all monies paid on options will be applied to the purchase price.

Maybe an option is not a possibility. The owner says, "Look, I'll sell but I'm not interested in uncertainty. You can walk away from an option, but a sales agreement gives me something to plan around and a definite time line to work from." You can't persuade him that this is a preposterous attitude on his part. After all, it is his property and he doesn't *have* to do *anything*.

You *want* the property. Everything about it looks good. What do you do? Well, first, and quickly, talk to your banker. Ask his opinion. If it concurs with yours, discuss some short-term interim financing. You may not need it (your sales agreement will provide a sixty-to ninety-day—more if you can get it—lead time for closing, within which period you might be able to get a permanent loan commitment), but your banker will understand that the possibility exists and—if he thinks well of the idea—will be sympathetic.

Remember that banks are not in the long-term financing business. Savings and loan institutions and insurance companies provide the fifteen- to thirty-year money, but banks, with their short-term help, can provide the bridge from sale time to permanent loan closing.

As you become more and more involved, in more and more acquisitions, you will find that financing gets easier and easier (always assuming that you have not established a pattern of slackness in meeting repayment schedules).

Your sales agreement will provide for such items as proration of taxes, rents, and other income and expense items as of the closing date and will, as I've indicated, give you a reasonable time for title search, making financial arrangements, and so on. In most situations, you would want as much time as you can get, remembering that you can close earlier if that kind of fortunate need arises (as where you have a tenant who wants to rent that vacant space in the little shopping center you are contracting to buy).

Naturally, your sales agreement will have a sufficiency of protective language in your behalf. Leases must be as represented, and so must expenses. You will have a right to look at seller's records in verification of his representations in these regards.

Every case will be different, but as a standing proposition, it is reasonable to assert that if the banker is optimistic, you should be too.

Four
Buying Raw Land

For value appreciation potential, raw land has it all over the already developed kind. The value of income property tends to range within standards established by gross rentals and cash flow.

Raw land has no rents and no cash flow. It has no tax-shelter benefits either, at least not to you (it might have some to its present owner if he is using it for farm purposes). Unless buyer has a specific use in mind when he acquires the property, he is betting on the future. We've already noted that, as a rule, developers or companies with need for real estate don't maintain their own land banks. They move into the marketplace and acquire what they need, when they need it. In a sense, as the owner of usable undeveloped property, you're their land bank. They will decide where they want to go, and then they will send their land experts in quest of a particular site. It matters not whether you have listed your property for sale (we never have) or placed a sign on it (we've never done that, either). If your location is palatable, prospective purchasers will determine from the public records (tax office or public registry) who owns it and will get in touch with you.

Indeed, there may be some psychological sales advantage in not placing signs on your land. In the first place, if you do emblazon it in this fashion and don't find a buyer, the "For Sale" notice, after some months of subjection to natural vicissitudes, tends to look downcast, as though the property itself might be afflicted with a problem. Passersby begin to wonder what's wrong with the land that it has remained unsold for so long. Of course, you can always remove the sign and say you hadn't wanted to sell it anyway. Signs also invite the curious and the rank speculators, who will call just to hear your price and then float that around the marketplace. Second, if you have no sign on the land, you can always act as though you couldn't care less about selling, even though you may be anxious to dispose of it—at least some of it. Your voice tells a prospect "no, no," or "maybe," while you try to camouflage the "yes, yes" in your eyes.

You should remember, however, that in buying raw land, the very reason commercial land users do not establish their own holding banks will work disadvantageously to you as well. This reason is simply the cost of carrying the property. When you pay interest and taxes you increase your actual dollar investment (though not your cost basis). Thus, you must at the time of purchase assume that actual market value will leapfrog over these additional cost hurdles. If, let's say, interest on your deferred balance and taxes equals

8 percent, in any one year, you're hoping that your increase in value will be more on the order of 10 or 12 or 20 percent. Usually, it will be. If you break the land down into smaller components, your value increase can often be calculated by multiplication rather than addition.

Let's look at an example, based, as are all the others used in this book, on an actual case. Let us assume that you, or one of your group, has located a tract of, say, 40 acres in what all of you feel is a prime growth area: close enough in to be needed for development in the reasonably near future, far enough out to be beyond the pricing influence of immediate demand.

Before proceeding, let us take note of two relatively immutable propositions in the otherwise frequently shifting sands of commerce in real estate: (1) Developers and others who acquire needs, sudden or otherwise, for land rarely have any in the deep freeze. They take their chances on being able to go into the market and acquire it. (2) People who own land with development potential are rarely able to hold it until full ripening. The time space between these two propositional outer markers is where you fit in.

Price

Let's assume that the 40 acres you want is near an interstate ramp and that none of the adjoining property has been commercially developed yet, although, as is the case with almost all interstate exit locations, ultimate development is assured. Let's assume further that, as is often the case with land so situated, it was originally used for agricultural purposes but is now simply lying there, unused, owned by an individual

who inherited it from his farming father. In our hypothetical case, the owner would like to sell, but is under
no particular economic compulsion to do so. He thinks
the property should bring $2,500 per acre.

Bear in mind always—and particularly when dealing in raw land—that no price is as negotiable as the
price for a piece of undeveloped real estate. There
may or may not be recent sales of comparable property
to serve as a measuring standard, but even if there
are, the uniqueness of land makes any other property
as distinguishable as one wants to make it. Tax values
rarely reflect market value, and market value is in any
event a vague and illusory concept. Legally, it is
defined as what a buyer who is willing but under no
compulsion to buy will pay to a seller who is willing
but under no compulsion to sell. The most experienced
real estate appraisers, presumably skilled and fully
conversant with this basic standard of value determination, can place widely varying values on the same
piece of property. This is demonstrated in courtrooms
all over the country every day, most conspicuously in
condemnation proceedings where a public body is
acquiring privately owned land and condemnor and
condemnee each bring appraisers to court to testify as
to value. Opinion differentials in these instances are
often astounding, even to one who has participated in
many such trials.

Value of raw land, in the final analysis, is what an
agreeing buyer and seller say it is.

A myriad of other factors are involved also. Does
the seller want his money now, or would he rather
defer payment over a long period of time? In most
instances, the seller of acreage property will prefer the
latter alternative, with payments of deferred principal
and interest to be made on a monthly, quarterly, or
annual basis for a specified period of time. Here again,

acquisition of raw land presents some unique trading features, since there are no margin requirements (as in the case of securities transactions) and no standard payout periods (as in the cases of, say, automobile or home financing). Whatever is agreeable to you and the seller is agreeable to the rest of the world.

But back to our case. Seller says he has 40 acres and wants $2,500 for each one of them. (A cautionary note before we proceed: Any contract with reference to purchase of acreage should contain language providing for determination of actual total land by survey. Seller may think he has 40 acres when in fact he has 38—or maybe 42.) A survey will be of value to you in any case, and the contract should provide for its being made and for a method of payment. Seller should foot the bill, but if worse comes to worst, you can split it with him or even pay for it yourself. Worse would come to worst if you feel the buy is too good to pass up and the seller is locked in on his estimate of 40. Your option or sales contract will provide that survey be accomplished during the time period for closing (and after option exercise), that a surveyor will be retained at once, and that closing date will be extended if his report is not received within the time established in the contract.

You have studied the land and feel that a price of $2,500 is not unreasonable, but you counter in the time-honored tradition of trading with $2,000 and ultimately agree on a price of $2,250. There is nothing mysterious about the bargaining process. Some people love it, others abhor it. Since there are no established prices for land (other than the price suggested by seller at the outset), it is an almost invariable part of the purchase transaction in real estate. The only exception that comes to mind is the sales price of houses or condominiums in a residential development.

I will just say this: Don't lose a purchase opportunity in raw land by haggling over a one-tenth differential. If the land is worth $2,250, it's worth $2,500. To put it another way, if it's not worth $2,500 don't pay over $1,250. If the seller in the case put says with vehemence that he will not take one cent less than his asking price, and you probe and test and find him unyielding and you believe his own valuation is reasonable, pay him.

The single best buy in unimproved land which our group has come upon involved a 60-acre suburban tract which for many years had been held in a family trust. The bank trustee, at the request of family members, finally communicated to the press that it was for sale, at a stated price. Because the family was well known, and the tract a prominent feature of the area, the offering received a fair amount of publicity and investors and brokers came running with discount purchase proposals. We made one ourselves, prompting a close friend in the trust office to call me and say that the price was firm, irreducible, and undiminishable. We believed him, and offered the full price, conditioned on 80 percent of it being financed by the trust over a five-year period (with payment of the 80 percent in five annual, equal installments of principal and 7-percent interest). Our offer was accepted immediately, leaving some other aspirants wringing their hands. The transaction has proven to be extremely profitable.

Financing

More important than the *price* is the *financing*. Here is where unimproved property offers its most tempting—and lucrative—awards.

Seller will, in most instances, want to avoid the

heavy capital gains tax incurred if he receives more than 30 percent of the selling price within the year of sale (i.e., if he receives 31 percent, he pays tax on 100 percent). His gain is measured as the difference between his basis (what he paid for it, or what it *was* valued at when he inherited it—if his inheritance came before December 31, 1976) and his selling price to you.

His capital gains predicament alone will dictate seller's preference for an installment sale. Indeed, this problem exists for seller in most real estate transactions and provides buyer with yet another negotiating advantage. In the case put, no brokerage fee being involved, and the seller being under no particular financial compulsion, it may be that as little as 10 percent down will appease him. He doesn't *have* to receive 30 percent, after all; he just can't receive in excess of that and still retain his installment benefit.

On a total price of $90,000, 10 percent would be $9,000, a tidy sum for one of modest needs, and he would be able to put in his lockbox a note and mortgage from you in the amount of $81,000.

You propose that your payment be on a ten-year schedule, with equal annual installments and an interest rate of, say, 8 percent.

Just for a moment, before discussing other possibilities, let's assume that you close on this basis. Your basic annual payment on principal would be $8,100, and interest would be on a descending scale, with the first year's payment $6,480, making a total first annual obligation of $14,580.

Let us say that your first venture involves four partners. The mathematics of this are simple enough. Each of you would put $2,250 at the front and need to be prepared for an additional $3,645 within twelve months from the date the transaction is finally closed.

Of course, you would probably option the property

originally for a period of sixty days or so, with an additional thirty days, say, for closing after option exercise, so that effectively you are controlling the property from the moment of option execution.

If you have some plans for the land in the foreseeable future, or for other reasons do not desire to put your own money at the front (as, for example, if you are holding a stock that is showing signs of good health), you might want to borrow your front $9,000 from a friendly banker on a ninety-day rollover basis—that is, with his assurance that you could renew the note each quarter over a period of, say, one or two years.

If you follow this course, you will have invested in the property only the interest charged on your short-term bank loan, but you will own and have exclusive control over an asset which you feel is reasonably valued at $90,000.

Release Now let's throw in an additional leverage factor. You visualize that you will sell the property in small sections. You anticipate that major oil companies will most likely control, if indeed they don't already, the ramp intersection sites and that their activities will generate spillover benefits to adjoining properties such as yours. Let's speculate that nine months after you purchase the property, a buyer contacts you and asks if you will sell 400 feet of frontage with 300 feet of depth, or a little less than 3 acres of total land. He offers you $30,000. Sounds great, *but* your land is mortgaged to the seller for $81,000. Thus, if you are going to take advantage of this sale offer you will have to come up with an additional $51,000 (plus accrued interest on $81,000) to pay off the mortgage so that you can convey clear title to the new purchaser.

Maybe your friendly banker isn't that friendly, even if you offer him a mortgage on the remaining real estate as security for an additional loan. Banks generally do not yearn for loans on unimproved real estate.

The answer to the problem, really, is that you should anticipate when you purchase the land that it will arise, not once but several times before your mortgage is paid off. Thus, you provide, in your original contract with the original owner, that he will *release* any portion of the property from the burden of the mortgage on payment of a stipulated price: for example in our hypothetical situation, $2,500 per acre (again, release pricing is a matter of agreement, but normally it is for a somewhat higher figure than the original purchase price; sometimes, too, seller will insist on a minimum amount of land for release, e.g., 10 acres). In the case put, you would—should you decide to sell the 300- by 400-foot section—tender (i.e., offer to give) seller the amount due under the formula (300 feet × 400 feet is 120,000 square feet, almost 3 acres, so let's just round out the amount at $7,500) in exchange for a *quitclaim* (release) *deed* to the affected parcel. If you were really sporting, you would provide seller with a survey and even offer to have your lawyer prepare the deed. It just might speed matters along.

There is another potential goody here, or in any case a provision that needs to be inserted along with the release agreement. If advance payments received by the seller would be sufficient to diminish, or defeat, his installment tax benefit (in other words, would exceed by some amount the annual principal payment), then monies paid for release should be placed into escrow, beyond the control of either party (*but*—and here's the bonus for you—with interest earned on the deposit to go to the buyer) until seller's next tax year. Naturally any such payments to seller would or could be a credit against your next annual installment, reducing it, in the case put, from the original $14,580 to $7,080 (or slightly less, possibly, since you would be entitled to a credit for some advance interest payment should the seller take out any of the escrowed principal deposit ahead of the annual payment date). The $22,500 profit on your sale will give you ample funds to take care of the difference and still leave you with money to put in another piece of land somewhere!

One word of warning should be inserted here. The Internal Revenue Service has recently disallowed an installment sale treatment which, as originally structured, met all of the tests for an installment transaction. The purchaser paid 10 percent of the price at the time of closing and the remainder was to be paid over a period of six years in 15 percent increments. The purchaser gave a note for this 90 percent balance, secured by a mortgage on the property. Subsequently, but in the year of sale, the parties modified their original agreement by providing that (1) buyer would pay the full 90 percent balance into an escrow account; (2) seller would cancel the mortgage; (3) buyer would remain liable on the note (although, practically speaking, buyer would suffer no exposure unless the escrow agent absconded with the funds); and (4) the escrow agent would pay over to seller the funds in the escrow account on the same schedule called for by the original sales agreement. The IRS rationale was that since the escrow fund now held a sufficient amount to retire the debt, seller was no longer looking to buyer (thus to the installment obligation originally created) but rather was now fully secured by the escrow deposit itself. Revenue rulings such as this are not binding on courts of law but nevertheless have authoritative status. I would strongly quarrel with this one since it seems to me the reason for installment treatment of sales transactions is solely keyed to seller's inability to get all of his money at one fell swoop. In the case put, he was as effectively barred from reaching the balance of sale proceeds as he would have been under the original installment agreement. Again you would want your attorney's or accountant's advice in structuring your own transaction but this recent revenue opinion at least suggests that if (1) you don't make all your installment and escrow arrangements at the time of the original transaction and (2) you pay all of the balance into an escrow account and thus procure a release of all of the mortgaged property in a single swapoff, you might—if you are the seller—be letting yourself in for a whole lot of trouble. Of course, if you are the buyer, any tax consequences of your purchase are not affected.)

Paying Interest Only   Sometimes a seller's situation will be such that he would prefer to let the principal remain the same and simply take down his interest. In our basic case, assuming no sale of any of the property during your first year of ownership, you would owe at the conclusion thereof $6,480 in interest and $8,100 in principal.

Two or three months before the anniversary date, if you feel a need to defer the principal payment, you might contact the seller, advising him that you are fully prepared to meet the payment of principal and interest as scheduled but inquiring as to whether he might simply prefer to receive the interest. This would leave his principal intact for *future earnings*. In the event the latter alternative appeals to him, you would want to stretch the note by a year; that is, you would enter a simple amended agreement providing that the original payment schedule be set back by one year. In effect, you are simply buying that time for an extra year's interest.

The Best-Laid Plans

As we have earlier noted, just as you can sue a contract-breaching seller for specific performance (or damages—it's your option), so the seller can claim damages (or compel performance) against a defaulting buyer.

Protect yourself against the unknown by putting a liquidated damage clause in the contract, providing for the forfeiture of your good-faith deposit (or the payment of some other specified amount) as your total liability to seller in the event you do not go through with the sale. Seller doesn't have to agree to this, of course, and if he won't, you will be confronted with a decision as to whether the prize is worth the risk. As a further protection, provide in the agreement that you may assign (sell) your end of the bargain to a buyer of your choice.

A final observation: Some states have statutes, most of which originated during the Depression of the early thirties, precluding so-called deficiency judgments where purchase-money mortgages are involved.

This means that if you have financed a purchase transaction with the seller, as is the case with the hypothetical transaction we have discussed, and you are unable to meet the payment schedule called for and unable to induce the seller to give you any extensions, his remedy is limited to foreclosure and his recovery to the price brought at the foreclosure sale. He may not proceed against you individually for the difference should there be a deficiency between fore-closure price and balance due on the note. Of course, if such a sale produces more than the obligation remaining, then you receive the excess.

You would at least want to know whether your state law has such a provision, but you should never enter any real estate transaction if you feel there is the slightest chance you cannot meet the obligations incurred on schedule. It's a fun game if you proceed prudently and within comfortable credit parameters for yourself and your colleagues. It can be more than a headache if you don't.

Five
Buying Business Property

The best way, or at least a good way, to find business property is to ask around. Ask the person who owns a property you like. He or she may never have seriously thought of selling but might be willing to liquidate. Of course, you will want to check with reputable real estate people too, but it has been my personal experience that the most attractive situations are often come upon just by asking around.

We have already mentioned that you can determine the ownership of a property by checking with your tax assessor's office. The sheer mechanics of this will vary from state to state and even from locality to locality, but in one form or another, you will find (a) a map of your community or neighborhood assigning block numbers to sections of real estate; (b) another, smaller map showing the specific block you are interested in and the individual properties that make it up, designated by lot number; (c) the name of the owner of each lot and the property's dimensions; (d) if there are improvements, a plot plan, showing the location of the improvements on the property, their approximate age and value, and, of course, the value of the land itself. You will also find the amount of annual *ad valorem* taxes assessed against the land and improvements.

Let's assume that you, or one of your group, has spotted a small neighborhood shopping center which, by most standards, seems well located. It has easy traffic access on two sides; it adjoins a well-established branch bank, operated by the city's largest banking institution; the surrounding neighborhood is well developed, with above-average commercial development north and west and first multi-family, then single-family residential south and east of the site. On a visit to your local planning office (where, among other things, you look at the aerial map of the area) you learn that a local developer is proposing to construct a six-story office building near the center, a most encouraging sign.

You judge, then, that the market which has supported this facility in the past appears locked in for the foreseeable future. Indeed, if the new office building comes to pass, it will be substantially up-rated.

The center itself looks a little shoddy, inferior in outward appearance to the properties surrounding it, and of nine storefronts, two are vacant.

Tax records reveal that the building has a total square footage of 32,360 and that it is situated on approximately 2 acres (108,700 square feet) of land.

Tax records also reveal that it is owned by an out-of-town company and is fifteen years old. The age is in your favor. Properties most apt to be available are those which have been in the same ownership for ten to twenty years. As previously mentioned, at some point within this range, tax-shelter benefits tends to lessen dramatically. At just what point will depend on the tax situation of the owner, depreciation schedules employed, interest rates and time of original loan amortization, and so on.

You write to the owner. If one of your group is a lawyer or real estate broker, always let him make the contact in behalf of your group (he, of course, will be a member of any partnership you subsequently form). Contact from a lawyer or broker assures the seller that (1) your interest is serious and (2) you have—or at least your representative has—some sophistication in real estate.

Let's assume further that the seller responds in due course, indicating that for the right price and to the right group, it (the seller turns out to be a corporation) would indeed like to sell the property.

Remember an earlier admonition. It is not wise to own investment real estate in corporate form. Perhaps the owners in our hypothetical case have learned this the hard way. A corollary is that when you come upon income-producing real estate, corporately owned, your chance of being able to buy it reasonably is often good.

So our owner corporation, as a further token of its willingness to sell, forwards an operational statement for the last three years (Fig. 1) and affixes a price tag of $400,000.

Tenant	Lease expires	Options	Annual rent	Overage factor	Overage collected	Tax escalation	Square feet
World Drug	12/31/81	3-5 yr	$18,000	2%	1,149	None	18,000
Mill Outlet	7/1/79	1-3 yr	8,400	None		Yes	4,200
Midway Advertising	10/1/79		6,400	None			3,200
Beauty Salon	8/31/80	None	6,600	8%		Yes	2,400
Finance Agency	1/31/80	1-2 yr	5,100	None		None	1,200
Pizza Place	9/30/79	None	5,145	None		Yes	2,940
Dr. Smith	9/30/79	None	5,100	None		None	1,200
Vacant							2,280
Vacant							2,940

Total $54,745
Overage 1,149
$55,894

Overage collected 1,149

Taxes 1976	Insurance	Loan balance =	Monthly payments
$5,700	$1,000	$150,000 (as of _____)	$2,859.92 (5.75%)

Figure 1

Financing

Shopping centers come in all shapes and sizes. The bigger the size, the more complicated the financing and operation. Here we are talking about a 33,000-foot center which, compared with a million-foot—or even a hundred-thousand-foot—shopping complex seems ridiculously small, but of course you can go even less than 33,000 feet and still have a healthy little cluster of buildings churning out profits for you and your colleagues.

Lease Strength   This brings us to another basic rule of thumb: The smaller the facility, the simpler the financing. A parallel proposition is that the smaller the center, the better the opportunity for increasing rents, and thus boosting return on your investment.

Long-term lenders (savings and loans, insurance companies) make their loan commitment on the basis of lease strength. If the developer has lease agreements with major department and grocery stores, supported by strong local tenants, he is able to provide the lender with the kind of security such money sources like. In addition to securing itself with a mortgage on the premises, the lender will require an assignment of the leases to him as an additional source of comfort. Of course, lessor will collect all the rents, notwithstanding this lease assignment to its mortgagee; lender's only recourse to them would be in the event of mortgagor's default. Once lender has its mortgage and its pledge of the leases, the project can be off and running. (Leases sometimes provide that tenants must approve a change in ownership. In any case, they will have to be notified.)

Overages   Most of the leases (all of the major ones) will be long-term (fifteen to twenty years, with renewal options); most will include the so-called overage provision, i.e., that tenant's base rent will be matched against a percentage of its gross sales revenues, with tenant paying whichever is the larger figure. (The overage clause protects the owner against inflation, while leaving the leasee with a relatively stable rent factor.)

The lender, of course, is not so much concerned with whether the developer gets extra revenue from its rent escalation formula as it is with getting its money back, along with the interest it has charged for the use of all that greenery.

No financing is going to be available to a large shopping center unless there are strong so-called anchor tenants. But on the other end of the scale, down in the territory where you'll be walking—at least initially—the situation is different. It is nice, but not usually necessary, to have that heavyweight tenant. You will perhaps have noted in the spread sheet shown in Fig. 1 that there is one such occupant—a chain drugstore which in fact paid a slight overage rental for 1975—but that the other tenants, all of them, are locals and probably not very strong ones at that. You will also have observed that only one other of them—a beauty salon—has any overage provision at all.

As mentioned earlier, the owning corporation, at least with respect to this property, had not been tending to its knitting. The property was poorly maintained and had never been really promoted. You, or a property manager with a little imagination and a paintbrush, could quickly and simply make it a much more attractive facility for potential occupancy by shops with overage potential. Here is where the opportunity for dramatic rental increments is presented by the small center.

Long-term leases are nice, but in some instances— and most particularly if your location is good and will be for the foreseeable future—short-term leases are nicer. First of all, you can take better advantage of any inflationary tendencies in the real estate market if you aren't locked in to a twenty-year lease; second, you can negotiate overages on a more favorable basis. The tenant, after all, is more concerned with rental as a predictable cost (e.g., not to exceed 5 percent of gross sales) of doing business than he is with the actual dollar amount involved. You, as landlord, can make the situation palatable to—or at least digestible by— your renter if you put his base rent at a level with which he can be comfortable and speculate with him on the growth which he should have in your location. His rent will never exceed a fixed percentage of his gross revenue. On the other hand, your maintenance costs, taxes, insurance, and other expenses will be rising during the lease term, and sales-percentage rent clauses will protect you against this inevitable inflationary trend.

An extremely successful property manager with whom we have had dealings tells us that he would much rather negotiate with small tenants for three-year leases than with large ones for twenty-year terms. He is able to get higher overage provisions with shorter leases. This is so because the owner is taking a greater risk (potential vacancy in three years rather than fifteen or twenty), while on the other side, the tenant is not locked in for a painfully long period should the location not prove to be a profitable one for his operation.

Note in Fig. 1 that the drugstore's overage factor is 2 percent. If the landlord had been attentive to his duty, he would have placed overage provisions in his other leases (particularly the restaurant, and the mill outlet store, where an average of 6 to 8 percent would not be out of line). Observe, however, that except for the drugstore lease, all of the rent periods are short-term. This tends to frighten a lender, but if you have done your homework in checking out the location, and are satisfied as to its quality, these brief rent terms will prove an advantage to you, as they did to us in the actual transaction.

They will be advantageous in two ways, in fact: (1) as bargaining leverage in getting a sales price you can live with ("You can't expect a buyer to pay your asking price with no more lease security than this"); and (2) to enable you or your manager to plan for better terms with, if need be, better tenants.

Formulating Your Offer

Asking price: $400,000. Gross rents for 1975: $55,894. Tax escalation (meaning simply that if property taxes go up during the term of the lease, the tenant will pay his share of the increase) was yes and no, and most particularly no, in the case of the major tenant, whose 18,000 square feet of rent area account for more than half of the center's total floor space.

Negotiating point: Overages should not be considered in computing yield for purchase purposes, since they do not represent a fixed income item. Only base rents should be considered. Thus, while gross rents were $55,894, base rents were $54,745. The difference in the case under consideration is relatively small, but in a situation where overages are substantial, they would become a significant factor in the bargaining process. The reason they should not be considered, of course, is that they are unpredictable both as to amount and existence. Of course, no rule is inflexible. If over a long period of time the same tenants have been paying substantial overages, these become facts of bargaining life from which no intelligent seller will be persuaded to turn away.

So let's take a look at where we are for starters. On

the base rent, and at seller's asking price of $400,000, you are looking at a gross yield of 13.5 percent plus two vacancies totaling 5,220 feet. Instead of viewing these as a liability, they should be viewed as a positive asset—again assuming you have satisfied yourself about location. A not invariable but usually accurate proposition is that retail rental varies inversely with the amount of space rented. Thus, you should get more on a square-foot basis for each of these vacant properties than you are getting for the drugstore property. Let's project a modest $2 per square foot (far less than a tenant could rent for in newly constructed quarters). We come out with a projected increase in base income of $10,440 per annum, raising our total base to $65,185. On this basis, and forgetting for the moment any expenditures needed to put the vacant spaces in rentable condition (usually the tenant will handle any interior partitioning changes—you should provide for this in the lease—and the owner any major repair work needed, as, for example, repairs in floor, ceiling, heating, or air conditioning), your return would climb to over 16 percent, and let's face it, you just aren't going to do much better than that as a simple matter of calculating return on total purchase price.

But how about return on investment? Cash on cash? Remember what was said earlier. The center is, for the most part, going to buy itself! Let's come back to that, figuring that we already have a good situation and that any improvement will be gravy. We will then be able to project net return more precisely.

For now, we have determined it's a good property, with an asking price that is not outlandish.

Information furnished by the buyer indicates that as of the date of its compilation, there is an existing mortgage with a balance of $150,000, monthly payments of $2,850, and an interest rate of 5.75 percent!

We'd rather not swap that loan balance with its low interest cost for a new loan with a 9-percent interest factor, although how to finance the project without paying off this old loan presents a problem.

Warning: Some mortgages provide that if the mortgagor sells the property without first obtaining approval of the mortgagee, the latter may declare the entire note due and payable. The reasons for such provisions are obvious. If, as is the case in our hypothetical situation, interest rates have risen substantially between the date of the mortgage and the date of the sale, the mortgagee will want to get out of this low-interest loan and into a better position. By refusing to give consent he can compel the new purchaser to refinance (or, in the alternative, defeat the sale, which still leaves him no worse off than he was).

In the case we're dealing with here, you have checked—through your lawyer—and determined that there is no such provision in the existing mortgage; that you may assume it and continue payment according to its terms, thus getting the benefit of that 5.75-percent interest rate for the full $150,000 balance.

Since the $150,000 is included in the $400,000 offering price, you are left with $250,000 (or whatever differential exists when you have completed the bargaining process) to come up with from some other source.

You figure that the seller will prefer a long-term or installment sale. This will almost invariably be the case where the seller has held the property for a long time and where his gain is substantial. The installment sale permits him to prorate his capital gains tax over whatever the installment period turns out to be.

You also surmise that $400,000 is a higher figure than the seller will actually take. Almost always, a first offering price is undergirded in the seller's mind by a lower selling price, although we repeat here an admonition delivered earlier: If your studies lead you to conclude that it's a good buy, don't lose the property by haggling over the price. In the present case, if the seller is one of those rare types who doesn't negotiate and won't back off his $400,000, then make your pitch on the basis of terms only.

But at the outset, anyway, try for a better price and terms you can live with. In the present case, $350,000 would make this property an excellent buy. Of course, you want to keep the existing mortgage because of its favorable interest rate. You hope that the seller would prefer an installment sale.

So you make him this proposition: $350,000 total purchase price, represented by assumption of the existing debt and $200,000 additional; with $50,000 of this amount to be paid in cash at closing and the remaining $150,000 to be represented by a note and second mortgage given at closing also, bearing interest at, say, 8 percent and payable within one year, or over a longer period if seller prefers. (By giving seller the option of term for the second paper, you have let him know what an absolutely splendid partnership yours is, and you might have lodged in his brain the notion that, well, maybe it would be nice just to spread this over three or four years.)

How did you come by the $350,000? Not too artfully, really. Usually, you would not pay more than 8 times the annual gross revenue of retail property (in the case put, 8×54,745=$437,960). This represents a capitalization rate of 12.5 percent (8 divided into 100). Whether you would go that high would depend on many factors, some of which have been mentioned. Is the property in excellent condition? Are the tenants healthy? Do their leases require that they absorb property-tax increases? Are there realistic overage clauses in the rent contracts? And, of course, most important, will the financing work out? Here, the seller's asking price is slightly over 7 times the center's base annual gross, better than 8 but not as good as, say, 6½. Six and one-half would give you a capitalization rate of just over 15 percent. Obviously you are working in safe territory, i.e., your purchase would be on a sound basis even at seller's asking price.

Your $350,000 offer is just below 6½ times annual base rents and, matched against seller's $400,000, still keeps you in the playing court.

At this point, perhaps we should inject another guiding principle on the sale and financing of real estate: *It is almost always easier to borrow on property you already own than it is to borrow on property you are acquiring.* This is especially true if you are dealing with a local lender—your neighborhood savings and loan association, for example. Somehow—at least in commercial transactions—lenders regard owners with a more generous eye than they cast upon buyers. Perhaps ownership connotes more stability. In any case, after you have had this property for a few months and spruced it up a bit, not to mention increased its cash generation by $10,000, you will probably find good permanent financing fairly easy to come by. In addition, of course, you can shop for money at a much more leisurely pace. Lenders—especially savings and loan associations—have a fluctuating inventory of available funds (reserve requirements established by state and federal regulatory authority determine when they can turn the spigot on). If you already own the property you can shop around for the best deal.

There is one more factor which can be given some weight in the permutation of your financing plans. In a time of easy money availability, you can often protect a very favorable loan, the balance of which is far less than the value of the property securing it, by simply getting a second loan for the additional funds required. In the motherly way that they have of denoting things, lenders call these "wraparound" obligations. Thus it may be that, if seller takes your counterproposition, you will be able to work matters out in splendid fashion, the while hanging on to that lovely five and three-quarter percenter. An offsetting interest factor, however, is that lenders will normally up the ante by a percent or so on the wraparound paper (e.g., instead of paying, say, 9 percent, as you would if the lender's position were first, you might be pushed up to 10 percent).

In any case, don't be foolish. Remember that your second mortgage—in whatever amount it finally turns out to be—will be coming up for payment in one year (assuming seller doesn't take you up on your kind offer to pay him over a longer time period), and you should have reasonable assurance *before you make final any purchase* that you will be able to handle this contingency.

In this mystic process of buying land, always remember that there are no hard-and-fast rules. So often, circumstances with which you never become acquainted prod a seller into liquidating his property at a price which may seem totally unrealistic to you and yet, viewed from his perspective, makes eminently good sense. Remember, you and he *are* the marketplace insofar as your transaction is concerned. Unlike the stock market or the commodities market, where such minor events as abdominal pains of a distant ruler can cause violent swings in price, you and your seller are just two people trying to buy and sell a highly visible, immovable piece of merchandise, almost all of the relevant attributes and liabilities of which are matters of public record or matters capable of external ascertainment.

To continue: You have prepared and submitted your counteroffer, adding a ninety-day period for closing. You should have reviewed the entire picture with your banker. There are many banks and many bankers, in your community as in others, but among all of them you should and probably do have one person and one bank on whom you lean for advice and to which you turn in moments of real financial need. That banker should be like your doctor or lawyer or accountant, an individual fully familiar with your personal situation, in whose judgment you trust.

The banker will appreciate your keeping him advised of what you're doing; he'll be flattered that you sought his advice even though he may suspect you're softening him up for a touch; and he will receive a sufficient education about the undertaking so that when you are looking for your permanent financing arrangement a few weeks or months later, he will be more disposed to assist than might otherwise be the case. In the interim, if he hears of money sources which could fit your needs, he might give you a helpful call.

Over and above all of that, if the banker says it looks good to him, that provides you with assurance about your own judgment. We reemphasize that for every one investment possibility you look at, the banker, through his customers, will have looked at a hundred. He may even have looked at the one you're discussing with him. Even properties which aren't shopped around (in the sense of being listed for sale and fondled by a large number of real estate brokers) are often talked around, and bankers are the first to hear.

Well, all right.

Making an Offer

As a lawyer, I recognize the importance of making an offer. Contracts, after all, require an offer and an acceptance. They also require what the law refers to as "consideration," meaning, in essence, that someone has to give up something in exchange for something else. If the seller accepts your offer in our hypothetical case, he is committing himself to you (and giving up his right to sell to anyone else), in exchange for your promise to pay him $350,000.

As mentioned earlier, this arrangement must be in writing, most particularly as far as the seller is concerned.

There are numerous ways of doing this, and your attorney will be aware of all of them and can possibly advise you as to which format would be best for you in the particular circumstances. All other things being equal, I much prefer a simple letter transaction, somewhat along the following lines:

Dear Sirs:

We hereby offer to buy your Queensland Shopping Center, consisting of approximately 2 acres of land and improvements and located at the corner of North and West Streets in Center City, North Carolina, for the sum of $350,000. We propose to close within ninety (90) days from your acceptance of our offer and to pay you $50,000 in cash at time of closing.

We understand that there is an assumable first mortgage on the property in favor of The Long Life Insurance Company and we will pay you the difference between the balance on that mortgage at time of closing and $300,000 by giving you a twelve (12) month note in the amount of such difference, bearing interest at 8 percent, with interest and principal payable at maturity. We will secure the note with a second mortgage.

This offer is based, of course, on your being able to

convey marketable title, free of encumbrance except as to the first mortgage which has a present balance of $150,000. It is also conditioned on all leases being current and as represented in the spread sheet you furnished us under date of _____.

Property taxes, rents and premiums on insurance policies would be prorated as of date of closing.

As an earnest of our intentions, we enclose herewith our check in the amount of $2,500 to be applied to the purchase price if our offer is accepted but otherwise returned.

If, notwithstanding your acceptance of this offer and your ability and willingness to convey a marketable title in accordance with the terms thereof, our client is for any reason unable to consummate purchase, you may retain the $2,500 transmitted along with this letter and neither party will have any further obligation to the other.

This offer will remain open for a period of seven days* from date of this correspondence. If the foregoing is agreeable to you, please indicate your acceptance at the place indicated below, keeping the original of this letter for your records and returning the enclosed copy with your corporate signature.

Very sincerely,

John Smith, Agent

ACCEPTANCE
We hereby accept the offer hereinabove set out.

X CORPORATION

By:_____
President

ATTEST:

_____
Secretary

*Sellers will often use one offer to solicit others. Therefore, as a rule, you should not leave your proposal open for a long period of time.

If the offeree accepts in timely fashion, and indicates as much by signing and returning a copy of your letter, you are in business. Of course, similar language can be employed if you are seeking only an option as opposed to engineering a contract of sale.

You can do all of this more ornately and should if the situation demands it. The situation might demand it if the project is substantially larger than the one we're discussing, or if there is a fragmented ownership, or for any other reason your counselor might feel applicable in a given case.

We almost always make the kind of simple offer referred to above and in one case were forced to bring suit for specific performance when, after signing and accepting, the sellers (husband and wife—always be sure to get signatures of all spouses where property is individually owned, even though the law in your state may authorize husband to act as wife's agent in dealing with their real estate) decided they wanted more money than we had offered. The property was a 500-acre tract, and during the period reserved for closing (six months in this instance, to allow for surveys and so on) an adjoining parcel sold for a considerably higher price per acre than we had agreed on. After suit was filed, sellers' lawyer advised them that they had no valid defense and we subsequently closed the transaction on the terms earlier agreed to. The process took about a year and in effect meant that we had effective control of the property for that time period without having put any money into it.

Controlling the property almost cost-free for this period enabled us to benefit free of charge from whatever inflation took place during those twelve months; it also gave us additional time to plan for use and financing of the land and even for selling a small portion of it when (as we felt certain would be the case) the suit was resolved in our favor.

Just to give you a comparison, Appendix 3 sets out a more elaborate offer, the kind that would normally be used in a purchase of substantial magnitude.

There are advantages to the letter approach. For one, it tends to keep the negotiations low-key. Sellers, and particularly those who are tentative about disposing of their property anyway, tend to be frightened off by heavy doses of legalese. A friendly, informal approach tends to allay these kinds of fears. It also sets a pattern for later cooperation in those dealings which must occur after the contract is signed. The lawyer's role in any real estate transaction is of vital importance, but it can be overdone. The ideal situation is for the parties to work out their own agreement, with the lawyer or lawyers around simply to issue advisories and of course to supervise the closing.

Earnest money, or the good-faith deposit, invokes another area of psychological concern. If you are dealing directly with an owner whose *bona fides* you doubt, it is best to submit only a small deposit. On the other hand, if you know the seller and have no concern about return of your advance should the offer be rejected or the title prove to be unmarketable, then you might want to go with the more substantial threshold payment: say, $5,000 in the case we have put. This tends to be convincing on the question of your own *bona fides*, as well as indicative of your financial stability, and thus is reassuring to the potential seller.

If you have arranged for a cash down payment with your friendly banker, he will understand your request for an advance of this kind; or, what the heck, you might want to be reckless and just advance some of your own hoarded funds until you know for sure that your negotiations have been successful.

Calculating the Yield

We will now assume that you have purchased your shopping center. Let's say that the seller countered your $350,000 offer with $375,000—thus splitting the difference between his original asking price and your bid—and you agreed on this compromise figure. All other conditions remain the same.

You have made arrangements to borrow $50,000 on a short-term basis and give seller a second mortgage so that you could, at least momentarily, retain the first mortgage with its $150,000 balance and its prehistoric 5.75-percent interest rate. The second paper is short-term, too, so you will need to begin your search for permanent financing within a few weeks or months.

Meantime, you have acquired your first business property; have rented, let's assume, the two vacancies at $2 a foot, thus increasing your basic rent roll to $65,185. If the drugstore produces any overage, you will of course do better than that.

Amortization on your existing mortgage is at the rate of $2,850 per month. Property taxes are $5,700 per year, and insurance is $1,000. Thus, you know that from your $65,185 you will be spending $40,900, leaving you $24,285 to apply to other obligations. You will have some maintenance expense, but since you examined the property closely before purchase and found its roof and structure to be solid and its heating and cooling systems working well, you do not anticipate any major items of expense in this category. Your main expense will be for cleanup of the parking area and you have found someone who will do that on a monthly basis for $150, or $1,800 yearly, thus leaving you with $22,485. These figures assume no loss of tenants or rents, naturally, but given the factual situation of your property, the risk of any lost rents or further vacancy is negligible, at least for the period of existing lease terms.

Your $50,000 bank loan is at 8.5 percent, so if it runs the full twelve months, you will pay your banker $4,250 in interest. You must also pay interest on the second paper in favor of sellers. You were able to negotiate this at 8 percent, so your payment would be 8 percent of $175,000, or $14,000. Thus you can readily calculate that your $22,485—assuming you let your temporary financing run for twelve months—would be largely consumed by interest payments, leaving you just over $4,000 for contingencies.

Expenses		Income	
Mortgage (per year)	$34,200	Rents	$65,185
Taxes	5,700		
Insurance	1,000		
Janitorial	1,800		
Interest (on $50,000 loan)	4,250		
Interest (on $175,000 loan)	18,250		
	$60,950		$65,185

Bear in mind, however, that the only interest you will have to pay within the first twelve-month period is in ninety-day intervals to the bank. Ninety days from closing you will owe the bank $1,062.50 (one-quarter of the total annual interest of $4,250). My suggestion would be that with this, as with any property similarly acquired, you use some of the monies available after meeting current needs for painting and fixing up. You might want to paint the exterior of the whole center, giving it a fresh new look. A sparkling new sign, perhaps with a list of tenants underneath, to replace the dreary specimen which was there when you bought it, would be helpful. There are possibly some small planting areas near the curb lines in which you might choose to place a few evergreens, easing the eye pollution presented by an unremitting expanse of asphalt parking area. Other light cosmetic touches will occur to you and, if carried off in good fashion, will boost the morale of your tenants as well as make the property a far more palatable dish so far as local lenders are concerned.

After you have done this—say, five or six months into your ownership—you should begin checking around for your permanent loan.

You talk to your banker again, reminding him that since becoming the proud owners, you have spruced up the project. You invite him to have a look-see, and he says he already has had one and compliments you.

He tells you that a wraparound might be quite possible so that you can protect your good interest rate on the first mortgage until it is paid out over the next five years or thereabouts, but that at least in-house, he is limited to a ten-year period for financing. You check with a savings and loan and find that it has some money for commercial loans and would be glad to have an appraisal done on your shopping center. You file an application for a loan of $350,000, stating that though you only paid $375,000 for the center, you have spent some money refurbishing it, as well as raised its gross income by a substantial percentage. You would like to borrow $350,000 because there are still other improvements you contemplate making which will enhance the property's appearance even further.

The appraisal comes in at $475,000 (or just over 7 times annual rental income), on the basis of which the savings and loan will let you have 70 percent, or

$332,500, over a fifteen-year period at 9 percent with 1 point ($3,325.00) as an additional charge for loan placement and due at closing. In part because one of your small group is well acquainted with the folks at Hometown Mutual Savings, you are able to persuade them to push that 70 percent up closer to the 75 percent which their house rules permit in such instances, emerging finally with a loan commitment of $350,000.

You settle finally for those numbers: $350,000 for fifteen years at 9 percent with a monthly amortization of $3,549.94, or a yearly total of $42,599.28.

If you close out the savings and loan transaction nine months after you acquire title (you acquire on January 1), you'll be confronted with the following figures:

1	Rents collected		$48,890.00
2	Interest paid to bank ($1,062.50 × 3)	$ 3,187.50	
3	Payments of principal and interest on first mortgage (9 × $2,850)	25,650.00	
4	Taxes ($4,275)* and insurance ($1,000)	5,275.00	
5	Painting and refurbishing	4,925.00	
6	Janitorial	1,350.00	
7	Utilities (exterior lighting and water)	270.00	
		$40,657.50	$48,890.00

*Yearly taxes, you recall, were $5,700. The $4,275 figure results from the fact that you prorated the annual tax bite. To simplify, we have hypothesized that you acquired title on April 1. Taxes are assessed as of January 1 for the calendar year. Former owner's fair share, then, was for three months and yours for the remaining nine (three-fourths of $5,700).

Thus you will have taken in $48,890 and paid out $40,657.50, the latter figure including all of the expenses you have been accruing *except* interest on the $175,000 second note in the amount of $11,156. You have $8,232.50 on hand.

But now let's project what your situation will be after the new loan has closed. Assuming that after paying the processing point and closing expenses you receive a net of $344,000, you will then have on hand a total of $352,252.50. From this amount, you will have to allocate (in fact the new lender will allocate it for you) enough to pay off the preexisting first and second mortgages. Let's say the balance due to clear out the first is $145,000. The second is $175,000. Accrued interest on the second is $11,156 (interest was of course current on the first, installment-loan mortgage). Totaling these figures, we come up with $331,156.

You will also—yes, there's the rub—have to come up with enough to satisfy the bank which was good enough to loan you $50,000 in the first place. You still have on hand—after deducting the $331,156 from the $352,232.50—$21,076.50.

Obviously, you have several possible alternatives: (1) coming up with an additional $28,923.50, (2) convincing the banker that his profits on the $50,000 loan are so handsome he'd be foolish not to continue it for another year or so, or (3) striking a balance between these two outer markers.

Your bargaining position is helped, of course, by the fact that the partnership account is with the bank and thus will provide that institution with a continuing, compensating balance to offset against your loan. Monies in your checking account, in other words, are available to the bank for loans to other worthy customers and thus for earning additional interest. This is a slight oversimplification but only a slight one.

Frankly, in this case, I would opt for putting about $20,000 on the bank note and carrying the remaining $30,000 a while longer.

While you are working on this, we will move on.

Cash Flow—Tax Benefits

Let's hypothesize the worst. The banker advised you that in his opinion you should pay the full $50,000. Maybe he simply wanted to discipline you against acquiring a feeling that all of this was too easy, or maybe you're in a tight money market; but for whatever reason, you have had to come up with the full $50,000.

This means, in net effect, that you have finally had to put some of your own money into this project— $28,923.50, to be precise. Since we don't want to completely clean out the partnership treasury, let's say that you put a total of $30,000 into the partnership and then pay the bank out.

Your investment, then, is not $375,000 but $30,000. Your cash-on-cash yield will be computed on the latter figure.

Let's see how we come out.

First of all, we will continue to peg rent at $65,185 per annum, though we know as surely as we know there are cows in India that this figure will inexorably rise—from overages, from renewed leases at higher rentals, from new leases at higher rentals.

We know that taxes and insurance and maintenance will rise too, but the odds are overwhelmingly in your favor that they will rise much more slowly than rentals. For the moment, since we are projecting income on current rentals, we will project expenses on current figures, too. Taxes and insurance costs are knowns. Cost of utilities—$360 for the previous year—

will probably rise slightly, let's say to $400. Janitorial is fixed at $1,800 per annum. And you figure $500 per month, $6,000 on the year, for maintenance (no history to go by here; the previous owner had apparently let the property maintain itself. The $6,000 should give you an ample cushion.). Thus, your expense summary would look like this:

Taxes	$ 5,700
Insurance	1,000
Utilities	400
Janitorial	1,800
Maintenance	6,000
	$14,900

Normally, a vacancy factor would be added, an arbitrary figure frequently computed at 5 percent for projection purposes. Your situation for the immediate future, with existing leases historically strong and the two new leases fairly solid, is such that I have omitted this item.

You are managing the property yourself (a simple enough task in a small center) and so have avoided paying any management fees. These would normally run from 5 to 10 percent.

So, expense items total $14,900 (with maintenance costs a pure guesstimate). To this figure we add amortization of $42,599.29, which results in a total outlay over the next twelve months of $57,499.29. Surprisingly, we will thus be able to project cash flow before depreciation of $7,685.71, for a return of 25.6 percent cash on cash.

I will not mislead you. This is unusually good, and I'm glad we could bring you in at such a healthy return figure. In any case, when you're out there on your own, you should, in today's high interest market, look for 15 to 18 percent.

But now we get to the good part. If you had bought stock with your $30,000, and could by some miracle receive that kind of return, you would of course pay income tax on that revenue as dictated by the IRS and your tax bracket. (You also, of course, would own only $30,000 worth of stock as opposed to the $375,000—$475,000 according to the savings and loan appraisal—worth of real estate you have acquired.)

With income-producing real estate, however, we add another dimension. It's called depreciation. As we noticed earlier, depreciation permits you to get a return of your capital investment in improvements tax-free.

Deduction for depreciation is allowed on the theory that the wear and tear of assets used in a business enterprise (in your case, of rent-producing improvements on land) is, really, just another expense of doing business. Thus, practically speaking, income is in fact reduced by the degree or amount of depreciation or diminution in physical value of these assets incurred in producing the income. The allowance of depreciation as an expense is simply to permit a taxpayer to recover his entire cost, less a reasonable salvage value, over the asset's life span. Although a bookkeeping minus, it's one of the big pluses for a real estate investor.

Six
Multi-Family Residential

There are many reasons why business property represents a more desirable investment object than residential property, particularly for the weekend investor. Most of them are obvious. Business tenants are more apt to keep up their own premises. Oftentimes they will improve them. They are not likely to awaken the landlord in the middle of the night to complain of a leaky toilet. They are not apt to have small children and dogs around the premises on a twenty-four-hour, seven-day-a-week basis. For the most part, they are solely responsible for the interior of their building. They usually stay longer. Except in office buildings, they do their own janitorial work.

However, we should not rule out apartments as

potential profit makers for the weekend investor. Indeed, your group might find apartments especially appealing.

Demand for apartments is strong and growing stronger. While national figures may be of little concern to you in your community, they do reflect trends, and nationally the trend in household formations is explosively up. From just over 63 million units in 1970 we have seen a dramatic but steady climb to almost 80 million in 1978 (as opposed to a net gain of only 10 million units in the entire decade from 1960 to 1970). A high percentage of these new households will be established in apartments. This demand is related more to changing life-styles than to changing population figures. Young people are leaving the family shelter sooner. In the minds of many, apartment sharing is less palatable than formerly. The rush to privacy involves—in part, it seems—a pad for everyone.

In this field, as with business property, we are postulating that you will start small. This is because you are weekend investors, not heavily laden with coin of the realm. How small? My suggestion is that you look for an apartment cluster of twelve or twenty-four units. Twelve units at $200 per month will gross $28,000 per annum, and twenty-four units obviously will double that—putting you in the rent range of the shopping center we talked about earlier.

In most parts of the country, you should be able to buy apartments for 6 to 7 times gross annual revenues. As we mentioned in the previous chapter, real estate people refer to this as rent multiple—"a rent multiple of 6." You can change rent multiples into capitalization rates by dividing them into 100. Thus, a multiple of 6 will give you a capitalization rate of 16.67 percent. The higher the rent multiple, the lower the capitalization rate. Generally, the older the property, the lower the rent multiple and thus the higher the return. Capitalization rate means, simply, the percentage of the gross return per annum on the total price of one's investment.

There is an old measure of valuation one still encounters now and then that rent property is worth 10 times its gross annual revenues. Under this pricing formula, the gross yield would be 10 percent and the net yield whatever remains after taxes, insurance, and operating expenses are paid. Unless the property is in impeccably good condition, with an unusually high short-run growth potential, do not—repeat, do not—buy on the basis of this pricing formula. Remember that the cost of money alone in today's market will be close to 10 percent.

Many factors enter the business of making a value determination on apartment property. Most of them are obvious. How old are the buildings? How stable is the tenant list? What recent maintenance has been done? What sort of heating and air-conditioning system is employed? How long since the last roof inspection? How desirable is the location? What are the taxes and insurance, and are any of the utilities separately metered? What has been the vacancy experience? Has management been used, and if so, how expensive has it been? What size are the units? How many bedrooms per unit are there? How much interior space must landlord maintain? Is there on-site laundering equipment? Are there storage facilities for tenants (such as individual basement bins)?

Look for a building, or buildings, with separate outside entrances for each apartment unit. These are difficult to come by among older properties, but in recent years there has been a strong trend toward the so-called independent or town-house unit. There are no hallways and stairwells to maintain, and thus there is no need for interior lighting.

Perhaps the largest single problem for the landlord with a modest number of units is management. There are companies in every community which will handle such properties. The going rate in our area is 10 percent—a healthy bite out of your rent checks, to say the least. These real estate agents will assume full responsibility for the care and maintenance of the property and, of course, for providing tenants. Most of them have carpenters and plumbers on call, and if emergencies arise, the tenants know to call the agent. Usually the tenants will not know who the owner is, even in a relatively small community.

My advice to you, however, is to manage the property yourself. Maybe a member of your or a colleague's family would like to be the contact person. Maybe you would prefer to give a substantial rental discount to a tenant who would, in exchange, be responsible for the day-to-day management of your project. Maybe one of your number is an amateur plumber or electrician or carpenter or all of these (as owner, you can, under the laws of most cities, work on your own property without having a license to engage in the particular trade, e.g., plumbing, involved—but subject always to having any major work meet city building-code standards). After all, there's nothing very mysterious about an apartment building. It's just a big house with a lot of rooms and thus has the same kinds of minor maintenance problems that you've experienced in looking after your own home.

If you choose your property well in the first instance, you will not have much turnover. When you do, there is the problem of finding a new tenant and showing a prospective renter the space. Again, you might impose on a tenant to look after just this narrow duty, permitting you to put a sign in front of your property reading, "Apartment for rent; inquire at Apartment 1."

Someone of your group must be responsible for ensuring that rents are kept current and bills paid in timely manner. Again, these are routine matters, but to avoid problems later, arrangements to handle them should be made within your group in advance of acquisition.

Most apartment owners require a lease and some protection against default by the tenant. There are various ways to handle this. The lease itself can be a simple instrument and of course standardized. Protection against damage to the property by tenants is usually handled through a security deposit, held by the landlord. Some leases require that the tenant pay the first and last month's rent in advance of occupancy. If the tenant vacates before one year is up, he forfeits the last month's rent. The kinds of insurance you can build into your lease will depend on two conditions primarily: (1) the supply of available apartments in your community and (2) the location and attractiveness of your own units. If they are near a town park, for example, or to public tennis courts or other amenities, they obviously will have more value and be in greater demand than apartments without such advantages.

Depreciation benefits are the same as for business property except that in certain government-subsidized programs accelerated depreciation is available to subsequent owners, whereas in business property only straight-line depreciation is permitted to other than first title holders. Apartments will also normally have personal property which is susceptible to short-term depreciation—stoves, refrigerators, washing machines, carpeting, equipment for exterior maintenance. These, of course, are subject to very short term write-off.

If you go into apartments, particularly within the size range recommended here (that is, twelve to twenty-four units), you should do so with a view to pyramiding your holdings. Again, the same growth advantages exist as is the case with commercial property. The tenants will buy the property for you. Your ownership of these first units will give you experience which is helpful both from the practical standpoint of educating you for increased ownership responsibility and from the economically realistic one of making you a better borrowing prospect. The best source of funds for apartment property is your nearest savings and loan. These associations are designed primarily to serve residential owners. They like apartment properties because apartment loans can be processed with no more paperwork than that required for a loan on a single-family residence and yet the return is considerably greater.

Apartment complexes in the size range under discussion are usually owned by small-scale investors like yourself, as opposed to the high-powered professional developer. They will come on the market for many reasons. Not infrequently, the death of an owner is the precipitating sale factor. Exhaustion of depreciation benefits is always a reason to sell, and for that reason apartments, like business property, would most often tend to be available after fifteen to twenty years in the hands of the same owners.

Do not be afraid of old apartments or run-down properties. If you will look about your own community you will unquestionably find, as we mentioned earlier, that some of the most attractive residences and apartment buildings are among its older structures. Run-down properties—provided the core is sound and other requisites, including good location, present—will often provide the best buys. Run-down properties in good locations will frequently be owned by out-of-state people who inherited them. They will be managed by a local real estate firm whose only concern (and, for that matter, instruction) is to keep them rented and send money. Often such properties are in the hands of a bank's trust department. Trust officers are frequently in touch with good opportunities, and you would do well to leave your name and calling card with some of your local fiduciaries.

Let's assume you have spotted a sixteen-unit apartment (two separate structures) in an older neighborhood. It is in one of those areas from which, but a few years ago, people were fleeing but to which many are now returning. As you drive around the streets of this section, you see abundant evidence of painting and fixing up, indicating that the national trend of moving back toward the center of things is showing local vigor.

The building you like needs considerable exterior treatment, to say the least, and quite probably the interior maintenance has been similarly deficient.

You check with the local tax office and find that the property is owned by one Mrs. Jane Roe and that the tax listing was signed by an attorney. Mrs. Roe's address is the same as one of the apartment's, suggesting that she is one of the tenants. The lawyer's signature on the tax listing would further suggest that he is looking after Mrs. Roe's affairs and that she might be getting on in years.

Subsequent investigation confirms this Holmesian reasoning. The tax records further show that the buildings were constructed in 1940 and that they occupy about two-thirds of the land. They are solid brick construction. The year 1940, you reflect, was a long time ago. Any buildings that old must have a large number of built-in problems.

You contact the attorney, tell him how you located his name, advise him of your possible interest, and ask if he knows whether the owner might want to sell her property. He tells you that she does in fact live there and has since her husband's death, that she is in failing health, and that he has been advising her to sell the property for some time. He says it's a sound piece of merchandise but does need some repair and renovation. The rents have not been changed for the last ten years and they are $175 per apartment, a total of $33,600 per year. He says the tenants—most of them, anyway—have been there for years.

He will discuss it further with the owner, try for an asking price if she is receptive to selling it, and will get back to you. You ask if it would be possible for you to have a builder look at the structures and inside one or two of the apartments, and the lawyer tells you he will arrange for that if the owner expresses interest in selling.

A few days later he reports back. Yes, Mrs. Roe might like to sell, but she would prefer to receive an offer rather than set a firm sale price.

The lawyer provides you with operational costs for the last three years. The builder looks at the buildings, and with him you look at two apartments. The buildings, he says, are sound. New furnaces have been installed within the last three years. The roof is all right. There is no central air conditioning, but window units serve each apartment. He believes it would not be too expensive to add central air conditioning, since the furnaces are fairly new and existing duct work could be employed.

A multiple of 7 would produce a gross return of just over 14 percent, and a multiple of 6, a return of well over 16 percent. Given the age and condition of the property, the latter formula is the one you should opt for, producing a bid price of $235,200.

You talk with your banker, giving him the history of the property as you have learned it, mentioning that you might want to pay him a return visit if negotiations mature and asking his opinion of the project.

He knows both the property and its owner and thinks well of both. Apartments, he points out to you, are currently in short supply in your area, and older ones will soon be at a particular premium for the simple reason that present construction costs dictate extremely high rentals.

You thank him and he thanks you. He would, naturally, like to have the account, and you, just as naturally, would like to work with him, too; in any event, and whatever happens, he will be pleased that you sought his advice.

You determine that taxes ($3,000) and insurance ($1,000) are not disproportionately high, and on the basis of this and the other information you have collected, you submit a bid to the lawyer of $235,000, conditioned as follows:

1. $23,500 cash at closing;
2. balance of $211,000 to be paid by giving an 8 percent interest bearing note in that amount to seller, payable over a fifteen-year period, with monthly installments of principal and interest in the amount of $2,016.45. The note would be secured with a first mortgage on the premises.

Your annual amortization on this schedule would be $24,197.40. We have already seen that taxes and insurance are running at $4,000. Janitorial and other routine maintenance will probably add $2,500 to that for a total of $6,500, leaving you $2,902.60 to play with. This would represent a return of 12.3 percent cash on cash.

Ah, but wait. Rents have not been raised for ten years. Mrs. Roe just hasn't bothered, but then, she hasn't bothered to paint or fix up, either. You are going to change this way of living. You are going to raise rent and refurbish. If you increase charges by $25 per month per unit (assuming that you'll lose no tenants with that increment) you will pick up another $4,800 per year, which will add to your $2,902.60 and bring you out with a total of $7,702.60, a vigorous 32.8-percent cash-on-cash yield. Of course, you *will* have to do the repair and renovation work, and thus, at least initially, the extra yield from increased rents will of necessity be contributed to capital improvement.

You feel that Mrs. Roe might like the idea of a fifteen-year annuity, and after all, $2,016.45 per month isn't exactly chicken feed. You decide that your offer is a fair one and that anything more will constrain you too much. You even decide that the fifteen years is not negotiable.

Mrs. Roe's lawyer counters with $275,000, but you stand firm and ultimately acquire it at your price.

Obviously, there are many variations playable on this or any bargaining theme.

You could have gone with $250,000, for example, which would have increased your yearly amortization from $24,197.40 to $25,974.84, and still have lived fairly comfortably with those numbers.

You could have proposed that no monthly payments be made for the first year, i.e., that you would pay the 10 percent down and start the fifteen-year payout twelve months from closing date. If accepted, this proposal would permit you to apply a good portion of first-year returns to repair work. This kind of proposition might have pleased Mrs. Roe, whose immediate needs would be more than met by the down payment even as reduced by the lawyer's extraction. She is, of course, fully protected by her mortgage, and indeed, as you improve her property you are improving the safety of her position as secured creditor.

You could have proposed annual payments as

opposed to monthly ones, which would give you a somewhat freer rein with rent collections although you would need always to be prepared for that twelve-month deadline.

You could have raised the price and lowered the interest. As we have mentioned before, you and Mrs. Roe and her lawyer are the marketplace and whatever you all agree on is what will happen.

A side note: Not infrequently, notes and mortgages such as the documents you propose to give to Mrs. Roe can be picked up before their expiration at substantial discounts.

Let's take Mrs. Roe, for example. She is seventy-six years old and she has two children living in another state to whom she will leave all of her property, which will include, of course, your note and the mortgage securing it. When, as she inevitably will, Mrs. Roe dies, her legatees might prefer instant to deferred cash and might be disposed to settle with you for considerably less than face value. You would make arrangements to pay them by refinancing with your favorite lender. As an example, suppose that when Mrs. Roe dies you still owe $175,000 on the note. For cash, her heirs might take $125,000 and run. It happens all the time.

Once you have completed the transaction on the Roe property, start looking for more apartments. Appendix 4 sets forth the basics for a sales agreement on residential property. Every community has its traders, and when word gets out that your group is in the market, you'll be hearing from some of them, as well as from the established realtors in your area. All of them can be helpful, but always remember, there's no law that says you can't make your own discoveries.

As you add to your stable, you will find that your maintenance and rent-collection procedures can be standardized. You will find also, as was suggested earlier, that financiers will smile more and more broadly at you as you enter their sanctuaries.

Seven
Single-Use Buildings and Franchises

Earlier I cautioned you against doing your own developing. Stay away from construction, I counseled. Just buy what's there. At the same time, I suggested that there was a permissible exception to this otherwise immutable proposition. In this chapter we explain what it is.

The largest category of franchise operations is the so-called fast-food category. Most of these operations feature buildings as identical as their signs. When you've seen one McDonald's, Arby's, Pizza Hut, or Long John Silver's, you've seen them all. Valid reasons prompt this uniformity. Some of them are obvious: standardized construction, better cost and inventory controls, more efficiency in operation, easier personnel training. Patron security is another factor. The customer likes to go into a McDonald's because he feels at home there. Whatever it might be, he has been there before.

Over the past few years these basic building plans have changed, however. Originally, fast-food service, at least in the sandwich segments of it, meant that you ran from your car to the counter and from the counter back to your car, pausing only long enough to pick up your bag of edibles and leave some money. In time, franchisors recognized that many customers might prefer eating on the premises, and this has led to redesigned buildings with so-called dining—perhaps better designated as "wolfing-down"—rooms added.

The point is that the building is designed and built to the specification of the franchisor. If he goes broke, or if for any reason during the course of your relationship with him he is able to void the lease, you could be in trouble, particularly if the building cannot be adapted to another use.

Leasing to a Franchise

First of all, it should be noted that in most instances the franchisor (Kentucky Fried Chicken, let's say) will not be the party you're dealing with. Company-owned stores—as these facilities are usually termed—are rare. You will be dealing with the franchisee, often a local resident who has sunk his life savings into the purchase of his franchise. It might also be a multi-store group, operating stores in a number of cities. Other things being equal, you're better off with the second type. They will tend to be stronger financially and heavy in the expertise department.

Leasing negotiations for operations of this sort can be very tricky. The franchisee will be working closely with the franchisor and usually will insist on a standard basic lease prepared by the latter's attorneys. These will run for pages and paragraphs and will tend to be weighted in the company's favor. If you have reached a meeting of the minds on the basic framework of the lease contract, then you will most certainly want to bring in your lawyer for the final stages of negotiation.

Generally, franchisees will want long leases and renewal options—a total time frame of perhaps thirty-five years (twenty years of base contract and three five-year renewal options). Many, if not most, such agreements are on so-called net, net, net formula, meaning that the lessee will pay for all maintenance, insurance, and taxes during the term of the lease. The Tax Reform Act of 1976 has made changes in investment ground rules generally which, in some situations, tend to make the triple-net lease less desirable from a tax standpoint than it formerly was. In such cases, it would be better to add to the basic rent an amount sufficient to cover the estimated cost of the three items. Your accountant will be able to tell you whether the Act might affect your negotiations with a franchisee, and if so, how, and you should definitely solicit his help before cementing an agreement.

Many lessees will try to persuade the potential landlord that if lessee carries the burden of maintenance, taxes, and insurance (whether directly or in the form of additional rent paid to you) then this will take care of the only future unknowns and for that reason obviate the need for a percentage override clause in the lease.

Under no circumstances should you defer to this kind of reasoning. An override is your hedge against inflation. Lessee will pay $3,000 per month, $36,000 per year, or 5 percent (at least) of gross revenues (exclusive of sales taxes), *whichever is greater.* Standard lease provisions give you the right to check behind franchisee's computation of gross revenues if you feel you are being fed erroneous totals. Generally this is no problem, and most operators—and particularly the kind you should be dealing with—are thoroughly scrupulous. They will drive the hardest bargain possible in the initial lease negotiations, but once the project and lease are facts accomplished, they will go by the letter of the agreement.

If you were to agree to a base lease figure with no override, you would still be receiving 1978 dollars ten years later when all of history teaches us that money inexorably becomes cheaper. If the lessee wants your location, he will generally capitulate on the rental point.

Land area required for a fast-food operation will vary with the requirements of the franchise involved, city building requirements, and so on. It will rarely be smaller than 100 by 200 feet or larger than 125 by 250 feet.

In any community, land values will vary enormously, but I think it can be safely said that land found desirable by a well-established fast-food operation will be valuable property indeed, appraisable for one-fourth or more of the total cost of improvements to be placed on it.

It might have been farmland when you bought it, but if a McDonald's or Arby's or Kentucky Fried Chicken likes a small chunk of it for a store and is willing to pay a base rent of $36,000 per annum, you can bet that your land has assumed another character altogether from the time when its original appeal was to a grazing bovine.

Its worth is measured by what it will produce, and once you have agreed with your franchisee, and if that lessee is financially solid, the land value becomes largely a matter of automatic calculation. This proposition becomes very important to you as you plan to work out your financing arrangements for construction of the building.

Earlier we warned you against getting into construction at all, and that admonition still holds. However, we feel that with a proper fast-food operation particularly, construction for a franchised service is prudent. The building itself, as we have earlier noted, is already designed. The franchisee will normally furnish complete drawings, and a firm contract price can be set. Normally, franchisor's building advisers will be on hand at various times throughout construction. Indeed, in many instances, they will be well acquainted with a builder who has built other similar structures and who is thus well acquainted with any architectural idiosyncrasies the basic design might possess.

We mentioned that the financial stability of the franchisee is of essential importance in a transaction of this kind, and you should leave no stone unturned in checking the lessee's background. Once again, your banker will be a valued ally. He may know the party well. If he doesn't, he can assist you in learning what you need to know.

If the lease is to be with a company owned by the lessee-franchisee, then—unless the company is well known and highly solvent—you will want to require personal signatures of the principals and their spouses in addition to that of the leasing corporation. This request will not normally be greeted with enthusiasm, and yet it is a common one and will be anticipated. Your response to their reluctance should be in words like "If you don't have faith enough in your undertaking to endorse the lease, why should we have faith enough to construct a building for it?" If they want your location badly enough, they'll endorse. If they don't, they won't.

Of course, if you can get an endorsement by the franchisor, you're almost home free, but this will not often be possible.

There are only a few franchises worth meddling with at all. Your banker can name them for you on the fingers of his check-writing hand. *Don't bother with the rest of the pack.* If you stick with one of these premier fast-food operations, your investment will be as riskless as an investment can be.

Construction

So that we can draw a profile, let's assume that the raw land which you bought earlier and which—you will recall—was near an interstate exit, has become interesting to a major dispenser of American-fried hamburgers and French-fried potatoes. When you bought—remember?—the land directly adjacent to the exits was undeveloped. Now two oil companies have acquired tracts and are in the process of constructing service stations on the property. In addition, there have been other developments—including an office facility and truck terminal—in the immediate neighborhood. You were wise enough to anticipate these kinds of happenings when you bought your property three years earlier.

Of course, you're still paying on the raw land, but recall that in your contract of purchase you inserted a provision permitting you to have some of the land released on payment to seller at a rate of $2,500 per acre. For the sake of simplicity, let's say that lessee wants 1 acre of land (209 feet by 209 feet). You can clear this tract from encumbrance by tendering your mortgagee $2,500. You would then have clear title to real estate capable—when a proper building is placed on it—of producing a minimum of $36,000 per year after all expenses for a period of at least twenty years ($720,000). The building will cost $225,000 to construct. If we put land in at $50,000 (with this kind of lease there should be no difficulty getting such an appraisal of value on your acre—just over $1 per square foot), you have a total investment figure of $275,000, on which your return would be $36,000 or 13-plus percent net before taxes and depreciation.

You will need good legal help in drafting your contract for building construction no less than you did in getting together on lease terms.

If franchisee has a favorite builder, who has erected this type of structure before, and he checks out well, don't hesitate to use him. On the other hand, you or one of your group might prefer to deal with a builder of your own choice.

Make sure you enter a firm contract, based on plans and specifications submitted by franchisee. Make sure you have a clear understanding with respect to personal property to be installed by the tenant (stoves, refrigeration units, tables, chairs, and so on). Have a written understanding with franchisee that if, at any time after the contract is let, lessee desires any changes in the original plans, such changes will be made only after lessee has signed a change order that includes the dollar amounts of the changes, these costs to be borne by lessee. You want your own liability to be firmly locked in at the $225,000 figure (or whatever the amount happens to be—we're hypothesizing $225,000).

In advance of all of this, you will have obtained a commitment from a lender, conditioned on its getting a first mortgage on the property and, probably, an assignment of the lease. This letter of commitment can be used to obtain interim construction financing.

Until the 1976 Tax Reform Act, interest and taxes paid during the construction period could be expenses. Now they must be capitalized. As first owner, you will be entitled to get accelerated depreciation; however, this is always a mixed bag, and whether you would want to speed up the depreciation process would depend, I would imagine, on whether you plan on holding the property indefinitely or selling it before you start getting penalized later for the speeded-up return of capital. Your accountant or tax lawyer will advise you on this.

Bear in mind in any case that depreciation permitted by the IRS reduces your basis in the property and thereby increases any gain or loss when the property is sold. If you use accelerated depreciation, you are confronted at sale time with its recapture.

Bear in mind too that with any income-producing property, and in some instances with non–income-producing land, you can always borrow against built-up equity by refinancing. If the interest market has not changed dramatically against you (if, for example, your original loan was at 9 percent and you can refinance at 9.5 percent) and if you need capital for another project, you can receive the borrowed funds over and above those needed to retire the existing mortgage, tax-free. There may come times and circumstances when you will want to do this. It is at least a factor to be considered among others in making your determination of whether to accelerate depreciation in cases where you are first owner.

Naturally, you can always cushion the capital gains tax consequence of any sale by going the installment route—accepting no more than 30 percent down and spreading the balance over a period of years. Your tax is then only assessed against that portion of the gain actually received in any one tax year.

Land Leasing

At the outset of this leasing narrative, we mentioned land leasing as one way to go and suggested that in some jurisdictions it is the main way to go. You can lease to or you can lease from. Why and when would you do either?

Leasing to   Let's go back to our raw land transaction, the 40-acre package, and make the assumption that your frontage is developing rapidly and that you are approached by an independent oil company which wants to put a self-service filling station on a portion of your land—enticed there, no doubt, by the existence of the major oil company's facility beside the interstate ramp.

The company's land representative says his people would prefer to lease the land for, say, a twenty-year period as opposed to buying it outright. He's very candid when you ask him why, telling you that his is a relatively new company in the field, that it is desirous of expanding as rapidly as possible, and that it does not want to tie up any more capital in land purchase than is absolutely necessary.

Makes sense and so does the company's financial report. The man is very direct with you. He says his company will pay you for land on either of two bases: (1) It will pay you a low base rent against a percentage (1 cent per gallon of gas sold), or (2) It will pay you a flat rental with provision for periodic cost-of-living adjustment.

The gross sales approach seems at first the more appealing of the two, particularly after you make inquiry and learn how revenue-productive such facilities can be. On the other hand, and just in your casual travels, you've noticed that service stations don't always succeed, that many sites are simply abandoned, and you would not want to be holding a lease of the first type should that happen to your location. The ever-present threat of fuel shortages also contributes to your wariness.

You decide to go for a fixed rent with cost-of-living escalator. How much do you charge? Customarily you value or price the land as you would if you were selling it and then charge ground rent as a percentage of such value. As an example, if you value the site at $75,000, and decide that 10 percent is a reasonable return for ground leasing, you would quote an annual rental of $7,500—and probably have your offer snapped up quickly.

This rent income is just that, ordinary income, with every dollar of it taxable. The lessee will pay taxes, insurance, and maintenance on his improvements and of course will get the depreciation allowance. At the expiration of the lease, whatever the lessee has put on the property will be yours.

In the interim, you will protect yourself by providing in the lease agreement that lessee will not subject the property to offensive uses—that lessee will not in fact (without the consent of lessor) use the premises for any other than the purpose defined in the contract during the term thereof.

Leasing from   It is unlikely that you will be leasing *from* except perhaps in the case of the fast-food franchise. In such event, you would naturally have to have a lease for as long as the period of your lessee's right of occupancy. For loan purposes, you would capitalize the land lease at least for purposes of getting an appraisal breakdown between improvements and land.

Let's put the case where building cost is $225,000

and your ground lease is based on a valuation of $75,000, with rental at 10 percent of that figure. Your total package for loan purposes, then, is $300,000. The lender, remember, will rely primarily on the strength of your tenant, but he also wants some assurance that if worse comes to worst, if the lessee fails miserably and loses his reachable assets in the process, he—the lender—will have some value in his security. Thus, he will feel more comfortable if your ground lease extends well beyond the period of any loan repayment schedule. For example, if the loan is to be for twenty years, lender would like your ground lease to be for, say, thirty.

Just as you, if leasing, would want some protection against inflation (either in the form of a periodic reference to the cost-of-living index or flat rental against a percentage of revenues), so your lessor will, if he is properly advised, want some assurance. For instance, he might charge you a base of $7,500 against 20 percent of any net rents you receive from the improvements you place on the property.

Let's assume that you agree on that formula and that your base rental from the franchisee will be $36,000 or 5 percent of gross receipts, whichever figure is greater. Let's assume, too, that franchisee will pay as additional rental a sum sufficient to cover taxes, insurance, and maintenance.

We have earlier discussed some strictures imposed by the 1976 Tax Reform Act on so-called net, net, net lease arrangements. Well, actually, the strictures are against deduction of interest on monies borrowed for investment, and ventures into net, net, net transactions are considered ventures of investment. The law says that—in some cases—unless you spend at least 15 percent of your rental income (from apartments, office buildings, fast-food franchises, and the like) for ordinary and necessary business expenses such as heat, help, repairs (but not interest, depreciation, or taxes) then you are deemed an investor (as opposed to the operator of a business) and you are limited by law to $10,000 per annum of interest deductions on monies borrowed for investment (as opposed to business or personal) purposes.

We will make the further assumption that you will be performing enough services and paying enough eligible expenses to cover at least 15 percent of your rent receipts (i.e., $36,000 plus overages, if any, plus amounts sufficient to cover taxes, insurance, and maintenance).

Your lender has looked at your ground lease (thirty-five years), your agreement with the franchisee (twenty-year base lease and three five-year options at figures above set out) and has concluded that it will commit to a twenty-year loan of $225,000 with interest at 10 percent.

Bear in mind that lenders are skittish about fast-food franchises. Unless you've got a McDonald's or Burger King or Arby's or Kentucky Fried Chicken, or one of a very few others, you will have problems getting a loan and you're probably better off if you don't.

The $225,000 at 10 percent for twenty years means monthly payments of $2,171.32, or a total annual payout of $26,055.84. You will also owe your landlord $7,500, bringing your total rental outgo up to $33,555.85. Remember that there will be additional rental paid you, based on estimated taxes, insurance, and maintenance costs. Let's put an initial round number on all of this of $10,000 ($6,000 for taxes, $1,500 for insurance, and $2,500 for maintenance). Your total-expenditure requirement of 15 percent will have to be calculated on the $46,000 figure, a total of $6,900. Payments for taxes don't count. Lots of luck.

Remember you're entitled to be paid for services

rendered, and of course you will have legal, accounting, and other administrative expenses. You will be providing janitorial cleanup, and in the case of a fast-food operation this is a daily and expensive requirement. You would probably pay the franchisee to do this. It is unrealistic for the government to contend that owning and leasing real estate falls, or even might possibly fall, in the same investment category as acquiring and owning stocks or bonds, but they have now said that in some instances the situations are similar and you therefore have to live with this artificially contrived similarity as best you can.

On the new building such as this you may take accelerated depreciation—up to 150 percent—and, for depreciation purposes, schedule a fairly short life—say, twenty-five years—for the structure. On that basis, depreciation for the first year would be $13,500 (4 percent straight plus 2 percent for acceleration, or a total of 6 percent of $225,000). The second year it would be $12,600 (94 percent of $13,500), the third year, $11,844, and so on. You can see how it drops off, but you can also see what a substantial expense item depreciation is to offset against your income. Interest on the twenty-year loan is another major item, in this case $25,185.84.

Let us see, then, how the figures work out:

Gross Expenses		Income
Depreciation	$13,500.00	
Interest	23,185.84	
Ground rent	7,500.00	
Taxes	6,000.00	
Insurance	1,500.00	
Maintenance	2,500.00	Total receipts $46,000.00
	$56,185.84	

Thus, while showing a paper operating loss after depreciation of $10,185.84, you actually will have a positive cash flow of $3,314.16 (expenses not including depreciation total $42,685.84 as against $46,000 total receipts).

Ground leasing is one way of traveling, in a manner of speaking, on the other man's capital. Everyone benefits. The landowner, who hasn't the savvy or inclination to develop his own property, can sit back and watch you do it, the while collecting a nice recompense for his ownership. You, if you play your cards correctly, will be able to build an income-producing property which, as the years go by, will become more and more profitable without *any* major capital outlay on your part. Of course, the franchisee will earn handsome profits.

Subordination

Another method of getting prime financing on property which you do not fully own (or, more accurately, own with the burden of a substantial mortgage encumbrance) is permitted through the vehicle of subordination.

Subordination, as the word suggests, means simply that in the event of foreclosure, the first creditor's claim for repayment will come second to the new creditor's claim. It is simply a way of agreeing in advance what happens to your creditors if the worst happens to you and you can't pay up. Obviously, to agree to subordinate, the first creditor would have to feel certain that, in the unlikely event the worst happens, there will be enough left after the other lienor is paid to recoup his loan. And if you are taking a second loan in order to make improvements on the property, chances are that this will be so. The property will increase in value, both from your improvements and from inflation, so that both your creditors can feel secure.

To assure such agreement, you must get the first lienholder to precommit himself. Normally this is done when you buy the property and always in a situation where the seller finances a portion of the sales price, with his security being in the form of a purchase-money mortgage. If the property is of such a kind and nature that you anticipate the possibility of placing substantial improvements (say, again, a fast-food-franchise store) on it before you have gotten very far with your annual payments, then you would surely want to explore the possibility of obtaining a subordination agreement.

At the time of purchase, you would enter a side contract with seller under the terms of which he would agree to subordinate his first mortgage (reducing his status to that of second lienor), *provided* that the new first lien is to secure repayment of monies borrowed to place improvements on the property, and *provided further* that the cost of such improvements will not be less than the amount borrowed.

Seller might also want the right to pass judgment on the proposed improvements, withholding (but not unreasonably) his consent if he dislikes the land use envisioned.

None of the subordination agreements with which we've been involved give the original seller the right of control over what we may put on the property, and it is best to stay away from this kind of condition if you possibly can. (Of course, if you can pull it off without *any* provisos, three cheers for you. Unless the seller is your mother, however, the chance of your being able to do so is remote.)

Provided the agreement *is* properly safeguarded, it can, like the ground lease, work for the best interest of all parties. It permits you to start improvements on the property before you've paid for it. It increases the value of the seller's security and diminishes the chance that you will default in your payments to him.

We have recently seen the value of such an understanding in connection with a large lot which we purchased in the central business district of a neighboring town. We bought the property three years ago at a cost of $52,000, paying 10 percent down and getting ten years to pay the balance. Anticipating that we might want to put a building or buildings on the property long before the ten years expired, we requested and obtained a subordination agreement. Conditions were that any monies borrowed on the property would go for improvements placed thereon and that seller would have the right to review all cost figures for construction, the better to satisfy himself that we would in fact spend the funds as the agreement required.

In violation of our usual rule against construction, we are now in the process of building a Williamsburg-style 15,000-foot office building on the land. One of our partners will be the main tenant and will pay rent to the partnership at the going rate. His need for more modern, more spacious quarters and insistence that our group provide them were the sole reason for this departure from custom.

The original seller has now become a second mortgagee and the improvement-financing bank has moved into first place. The improvements (all of which are being paid for through loan proceeds) are costing $375,000. Space not required by our partner has already been leased to other professionals, and the projection for rent receipts indicates that there will be an ample amount to make payments on both first and second mortgages, as well as cover other expenses of ownership.

The only investment we have in the property to date is the down payment on the land ($5,200) and two annual payments of principal and interest under the ten-year payout program to the original owner.

But for the subordination agreement, we would not have been able to accomplish so provident a result.

Eight
Office Buildings

Office buildings fall somewhere between shopping centers and apartments. They will give you more headaches than the latter and fewer than the former. Free-standing, or separate, office space is an essential of doing business for, among others, accountants, insurance agents and adjusters, advertising agencies, architects, attorneys, planning consultants, doctors, dentists, private detectives, civil engineers, consulting engineers, employment agencies, manufacturers' representatives, salesmen, mortgage brokers, optometrists, real estate agents, tax-return preparers, travel agencies, etc. The list may well be endless.

Let's say for now that a tremendous amount of business-building footage is dedicated to office use. It is much too big a market for the weekend investor to overlook.

Just as apartments and shopping centers come in all sizes, so do office buildings. The kind you should be interested in come mainly in size small and preferably in one-story models. A two-story building without an elevator is an anachronism, and a two-story building with an elevator puts you into an entirely different pricing zone.

After all, a modest 10,000-square-foot single-story office building, renting at a modest (by today's standards) $5 per foot per year will gross $50,000 every twelve months, or about $4,166.66 per month. I say that $5 per foot is modest rental mainly because you cannot at today's costs build new space that will rent as reasonably. The same goes for the $2 per foot we used in discussing shopping centers and the $200 per month we spoke of in talking about apartment rental.

As time marches on you will be able to closely trail the rentals of new buildings as they continue their upward climb. As new construction rents for $7, $8, and $9, you will be renting for $5, $6, and $7.

Generally, the owner of an office building is expected and probably required under the tenants' leases to provide janitorial services. No problem. Every community has independent contractors who do this kind of work for a fixed fee. In our community, this is often a family operation. The family swoops in, sweeps through, and barrels on to the next client.

Assuming your tenants are all of good caliber, rentals will be paid promptly. You will pay utilities unless office units are separately metered or unless a charge factor is arbitrarily built into each lease that reflects extra heavy use of one utility or another by the tenant (as, for example, of electricity by a radiologist).

Leases will usually be for three years, with right of

renewal and rental for the next term pegged at some mutually agreeable floating marker. Most often this would be the cost-of-living index of the Bureau of Labor Statistics for the region in which your city is located. At renewal time, the rent will be increased by the percentage of increase in the index from the date of the original lease. This should be phrased to have effect whether the index shows an increase or decrease, but, be assured, it will most likely show an increase. You might try for a tax escalator, too (tenant to bear his pro rata part of any *ad valorem* tax increase assessed after the date of original lease), but you will find opposition in some quarters from tenants who will complain that the cost-of-living barometer is designed to cover increased landlord expenses, including tax boosts. Your answer is the obvious one: The cost-of-living reference is to cover increased building-maintenance costs. It's to pay for janitors and plumbers and carpenters and material suppliers. Tax assessment is another matter altogether, involving government action in a field over which you have no control. You know what that action has resulted in when you sign a new lease, but beyond that you're in the hands of fate.

With office structures, as with the other types we've discussed, you will want to make as thorough an advance inspection as possible. Get the same reliable builder (or other individual knowledgeable in construction) who advised you on the shopping center and apartment properties.

Make sure that there are enough bathrooms to meet current building-code standards. You cannot be compelled to add bathrooms unless and until you seek at some later time to add to or modify your building. At that time the city inspector might require that you bring bathrooms up to existing code standards (probably toughened since your building was originally constructed) as a condition of issuing the add-on building permit. He might be on dubious legal ground in doing this, but at least he can cause you concern. It is difficult to find extra space for bathrooms in existing office buildings. Check with particular care the heating and air-conditioning equipment. Inquire of current tenants as to their state of contentment with these systems. As always, have a knowledgeable expert check the roof.

Remember that short of natural disasters—hurricanes, earthquakes, disturbances of that sort—a well-constructed building will last a very long time. It may become *functionally* obsolescent, but that is another story you will not need to be concerned with if you buy prudently in the first instance. As an illustration, an office building without a central cooling system—particularly if such a system could not be efficiently installed—would be functionally obsolete in today's market. You should not buy such a building in any case.

Let's get back to another hypothesis, this time injecting a new factor, viz., brokerage.

By now, word has gotten out in some quarters of the professional real estate fraternity that your little group is in the market. You have become a prospect and you will be regularly contacted when commercial properties come on the market.

In this instance, an agent named Brick Mortar has called one of your members who is known to him and advised that he, Brick, has listed a first-rate office property, located near a medical park, containing 11,000 square feet of rentable space (all but 2,000 of which is currently rented) and spinning off a gross take—when fully occupied—of $44,000 per year. It is underrented, says Brick, but Old Doc Suture, who built it originally and who has recently retired and moved to Fort Lauderdale, just hasn't pushed the rent charges up the way he should have.

As we have previously mentioned, this frequently turns out to be the case with older property. The owners have not boosted rents to the degree that changing market conditions warrant. It is an omission which you should always take advantage of in the bargaining process. Notwithstanding Brick Mortar's perception that the rents are too low, the fact remains that those are the rents. You are obliged to honor them at least for the term of existing leases, and they are the only returns this particular piece of the market has ever generated.

Note: When you sell property, don't emulate Old Doc Suture. Before even breathing sale to anyone, be sure that the property is in first-class condition, that the rents are in line with the current market insofar as it is possible for you to make them so, and that all of your rentable space is occupied.

Brick provides you with an operational statement for the past three years and tells you that the price of the property is $440,000, observing as he does so that when the 2,000 square feet of unrented space is tenanted—at maybe $5 per square foot—you will be looking at a gross yield of $46,800.

Heretofore you have been very fortunate. You bought your land directly from the owner. You did the same with the shopping center, through a stroke of luck that will not follow you everywhere. The apartments were also acquired from the owner, albeit through the intermediation of her counselor. Now another economic factor enters the purchase equation: brokerage fee.

Doc Suture, the seller, has listed the property with Brick Mortar and agreed to pay Brick or his agency a fee, ranging from 5 to 10 percent of the sales price. At first blush this does not seem to affect you. In fact, however, it affects you very directly, because Old Doc Suture is going to build that fee into his sales price and, worse, Brick—understandably—is going to want it at the front. You might defer everything else in some cases, but not the realtor's fee.

It's apparent that Brick and his client are operating under the ancient measuring standard—earlier described—of arriving at value through multiplying annual rents by 10. In this case, $44,000 of rent equals $440,000 of value.

The subject of price and how arrived at is endlessly fascinating, whatever the commodity involved. It is especially so with real estate because of the absence of prescribed parameters. Again, in this case as in the others we've discussed and as in all the cases in which you'll be involved (unless you're buying at an auction sale), the price is what you and Old Doc can agree upon.

For openers, you might get Brick's attention by suggesting that the price here is so totally absurd it would be pointless to respond to it with a counteroffer.

"Never know till you try," says Brick.

"We'll let you know," you say. "Don't call us, we'll call you."

Even if you want the property very much, cool it. Let Brick sweat. He is probably more anxious to sell than Doc. Meantime, learn what you can about the Sutures. Why did he retire? Why did they move to Fort Lauderdale? How old is he? How about Mrs. Suture? What's her story? Check the public records to see if they own any other real estate in town.

Wait for Brick's call, which, be assured, will come ultimately, notwithstanding your admonition.

"Why don't you guys make Old Doc an offer?" Brick suggests. "Nothing ventured, nothing gained. Give me something in writing, a little deposit, and I'll see what he says. What've you got to lose?"

"We're looking at another property over in that area." You can almost see Brick's ears perk up.

"Not the Armbruster building, is it?"

"Wouldn't want to say."

"Make me an offer."

"We'll see."

Of course, Brick is talking with everyone else he can think of, and before you come back to him with an offer, the property may be under option or sales contract. If it is, so be it. There will always be other office buildings for sale, even though they may not be as pretty as this one with its whitewashed brick, green shutters, green hipped roof, and the poplar and white pine around the perimeter of its parking area.

You talk to your banker. He knows the building and likes it and suggests that you might want to at least try for an option at a reasonable price.

Your intelligence gathering operation on the Sutures has produced a fair measure of information. Doc was a GP, patient and kindly, an old school practitioner who made good money almost in spite of himself. He and his wife were childless and lived simply. He was not to be ranked among the wealthiest medicos in town, but was comfortably off, with an adequate retirement annuity. He owns no other property in town.

This is good news and bad news. The bad news is that there is probably not the slightest compulsion on Doc to sell—unless (a rather unlikely prospect at his age) he wants to buy some business property in Fort Lauderdale. The good news is that he might be interested in doing some long-term financing himself.

You review the operational statement. Pending lease expirations, and assuming you can rent up the vacant space at $5 per foot: $46,000.

Annual Expenses		Annual Income	
Taxes	$ 8,500	Total rents	$46,800
Utilities	3,500	Less: Expenses	19,200
Janitorial	2,000		$27,600
Maintenance	4,000		
Insurance	1,200	Monthly Income	
	$19,200	$27,600 ÷ 12 = $2,300	

Expenses, then, a total of $19,200 (with the only play being in your estimate of maintenance expense), are offset against income with a difference of $27,600. Expenses bite off 41 percent of income, leaving you with just under 60 percent for amortization and contingencies.

Maybe you can work backwards on this one. If someone were foolish enough to pay the $440,000, his net return would be 6.3 percent—largely sheltered to be sure, but scarcely if any better than he could do with tax-free municipals. Indeed if we threw in another 5 percent for management, thus adding another $2,300 to expense, and realistically assumed some vacancy— let's say again 5 percent for another $2,300—we would add $4,600 to expenses. This would reduce net to $23,000 and yield percentage to 5.3 percent. Except in the kind of situation we've mentioned earlier, superior property with immediate value growth potential, most real estate investors would not opt tor so low a return.

So let's see what kind of amortization that $27,600 will support (again noting that we're assuming owner management and good fortune in keeping the place fully rented). For openers, we look at a prime loan of $250,000.

We check the tables, or do our own calculation, projecting a 9 percent interest rate and looking at payout periods of ten, fifteen and twenty years.

Payout period	*Monthly*	*Yearly*
10 years	$3,166.90	$38,002.80
15 years	2,535.68	30,428.16
20 years	2,249.33	26,991.90

Only the twenty-year program (assuming a 9-percent interest factor always) would get you under your monthly net before depreciation of $2,300, an annual $27,600, and this is assuming you are only borrowing $250,000. Old Doc, remember, wants $440,000 total.

Through all your calculations bear in mind that the building is underrented. We're postulating that you can up the yield in the unrented 2,000-square-foot portion to $5 per square foot immediately, but you should also be able to increase your current intake as leases come up for renewal on the other 9,000 feet, since $4 is below market for this type of building. Thus, and on a staggered basis over the next two years, you should be looking at a minimum of $9,000 more per year for a total rent roll of $54,000 instead of the $46,800 we've been playing with. This means, from your standpoint, that you can cut it awfully close during the early going. Using the rule of thumb for figuring total value at 6½ to 7 times the current rents, you'll be looking at a value range of $300,000 to $320,000.

There is still another technique which we have not yet explored and that might well appeal to Doc Suture. For want of a better term, I suppose, it is often referred to as balloon financing. It involves paying on a long-term amortization schedule with a shorter-term obligation to wipe out the debt. For example, you might propose to a purchaser—in this case the venerable doctor—that you will pay for ten years on the twenty-year amortization schedule of payment and that at the completion of the tenth year you will pay the full balance in a lump sum.

This approach might have several appeals to the seller, particularly one situated like Brick Mortar's client. Ten years is within his life expectancy, and there is a certain psychological value in this. He may live for twenty years, but there is greater certainty that he will make it for another ten. The monthly income of $2,249.33 in the interim is not to be sneezed at, and after ten years he'll get the balloon, which will turn out to be something like $177,500.

From your standpoint, the property would undoubtedly have increased in value during that period and you would probably be able to borrow considerably more than the amount needed to deflate the balloon. You might want to do this to put some tax-free revenue in your pocket.

All of the foregoing speculation about offering alternatives is based on an assumption that Doc Suture will take some financing paper. We have earlier noted the advantages to you when the owner will finance the sale of property.

Again, as in all of your earlier transactions, you have thoroughly checked the building and the market. You must also go over the possibilities with your banker, remember. After all, you will be needing some front cash. He may tell you to get off his back, notwithstanding the fact that you are fully complying with your current obligations to him. He would do this laughingly, of course, but he would mean it.

Here we remind you of a caveat expressed earlier: Have more than one friendly banker. Preferably, have three or four friendly bankers. What one will do for you at a given time, another won't. Banks are as different in their approach to doing business as any other kind of enterprise, notwithstanding the display of conservative uniformity they generally manage to convey to the public, and naturally, the loan capacity will vary from time to time and bank to bank! One of your colleagues might have traditionally done business with Fifth National; another one, with Center City Trust Company; another one, with the River Bank. At one time or another, use them all.

Admonition: Always do what you tell a banker you'll do. He has put faith in you, and he is answerable to someone else who calls him to account just as you are called to account. He knows he'll never make senior vice-president if he is putting the bank's money on some congenital delinquents. Don't let him down. If you are supposed to make a payment on principal on February 15 and you know on February 1 that you will not be able to meet that payment but that you will be able to keep the interest current and will be able to double up at the end of your next ninety-day period in May, then go by early and discuss it with the man. Explain the facts fully. *Call him; don't make him call you.*

Your credit standing does not show up on your balance sheet, but it is one of the most important aspects of your potential net worth. A good credit standing is a substantial asset and absolutely essential if you are going to make a fortune (small or large) in real estate.

In many years of dealing with bankers, I have invariably found them to be understanding. What they ask of you is really a very cheap commodity: good faith.

Whichever of your bankers you wind up with, lay

it out for him. Tell him about the low rents and your plans for raising them as current leases (all of which are short-term) expire. Discuss your idea about seller financing, including the ballooning formula. Tell him you feel the property is worth $300,000 to $320,000 and that you would like to submit an offer within that range, with front cash of $50,000. Where will you get the $50,000? he wonders. You were hoping to get it from him, you respond, for a period of, say, two years, with interest payable quarterly, and with the bank secured—if it wants more than your endorsements—by a second mortgage on the building.

In the interim, you will be doing some refurbishing of the offices (exterior painting, mainly) and some landscaping.

Of course, you will place the partnership account with his bank, thus providing it with a new customer and a modest, if fluctuating, checking account.

The banker has your personal statements (if they're not current, he'll ask you to update them), and these, remember, are looking better all the time. In preparing financial statements for a bank (or any other institution, for that matter), maintain your integrity. Be scrupulously objective, most particularly about your land holdings. A side comment: Be sure that your and your partners' valuations agree.

Any property you have bought should have equity value to you. If it didn't, you wouldn't have bought it. As an example, if you pay Doc Suture $300,000 for this building, all of it borrowed ($250,000 from Doc, say, and another $50,000 of temporary financing from the bank), it is because you felt the building was worth more than that to you. With a $54,000 rent roll, instead of the current $44,000—and even your immediately-hoped-for $46,800—the building picks up another $50,000 or so in value, and if you anticipate getting into these fairly soon, then you can in all good conscience show an equity of $50,000 in the partnership.

The banker likes your idea. On the terms mentioned, he'll let you have the $50,000.

All right, then. We are now ready to call Brick Mortar. It's offer time. Ring the bells. Offeror to offeree, here's some money, sell to me. After final discussions you have decided to reduce the interest proposal to 8 percent, not a bad return on a secured paper. The 1-percent saving over the original 9 percent considered will make a substantial difference.* You word it up, simply, engagingly, legally.

Dear Mr. Mortar:

We hereby offer to purchase the 11,000 square foot office building of your client, Dr. M. D. Suture, located at the corner of X and Y Streets in Center City for $300,000, payable as follows:

1. $50,000 cash as closing;
2. Balance of $250,000 evidenced by note payable in ten years, on a twenty year amortization schedule bearing interest at the rate of eight percent per annum and secured by a purchase money mortgage. Buyer would have right of prepayment without penalty.†

*On a twenty-year pay schedule, $2,091.13 per month and $25,093.50 per year as against $2,249.33 and $26,991.90 respectively.

†Prepayment, as the word suggests, means paying off the loan before its due date. In the absence of such a provision, and assuming you wanted to pay the note before maturity, the seller could demand full interest based on the terms of the note, under the so-called benefit of bargain principle. If interest rates had dropped since the original note was given, or in any case if sellers felt they could not find as attractive a secured investment in the marketplace, it might be to their advantage to insist on enforcement of the instrument as written. They could not do so, however, if borrower-buyer had the right of "prepayment without penalty."

We would like to close within 120 days of your client's acceptance of this offer.

As good faith deposit, we enclose our check in the amount of $5,000 to be credited on purchase price if the offer is accepted.

Of course, all of this is conditioned on your client's being able to convey a good fee simple, marketable title, free from all encumbrances.

If the foregoing is agreeable, please have Dr. and Mrs. Suture sign at the place indicated below, returning the enclosed copy for our file.

Very truly yours,

_____

Agent

On this _____ day of _____, 1978, we accept the above offer subject to all its terms and conditions.

_____

_____

I suppose now you want to know how it turns out. Well, you ultimately purchase at $310,000, $50,000 down, a balloon after ten years on a twenty-year payment schedule, and interest at 8 percent. Your monthly payment is $2,174.77 and your annual, $26,-097.24. With increased rents, you are able to live with the project quite comfortably and to pay the interest on your second paper at the bank. Eventually (in ten years) you will have to resolve that problem, but you have ample time and—presumably, by now—ample resources (financial and mental) to accommodate to that. Meantime, you're the owner of your first office building and as of now have yet to invest your first out-of-pocket dollar in the enterprise.

Nine
Larger Transactions

Up to now, the most expensive project we've talked about has been the shopping center at $375,000.

Just for comparison's sake, let's take a look at a somewhat larger transaction. Again, we will base this example on an actual case.

You will remember that our first center had about 33,000 square feet of rentable area and minimum income (no vacancies, no overages) of $65,000 per year. We will now consider the purchase of a larger property, this one with 51,565 rentable feet and a base rent-roll production of $103,500. In the year preceding your negotiating to buy the property, it produced an additional $13,000 in overages, for a total rent of $116,500.

The property is held by a partnership (three individuals), and one of the partners has recently died. The remaining partners—and the heirs of the deceased partner—want to sell. They are asking $825,000. The total site consists of 3 acres, and almost all of the surrounding property is fully developed.

You look at the center and you like what you see. The tenant mix is good, and on inquiry you learn that two of the three anchor tenants (the supermarket and the variety store) still have long periods remaining on their leases. The property is about fifteen years old.

Figure 2 tells the story on lease terms, rents, overages, footages, and provisions for tax escalation. It does not reflect anything for utilities and maintenance reserves, and of course it is assuming a fully rented facility. In making your own projections, you will naturally build in allowances for maintenance, utilities, and vacancies (usually estimated at 5 percent per annum for the total property).

Remember, in making your calculations of value you will not consider the excess rentals received but only the base rent as guaranteed under the leases. You do this because (a) your lender will not consider them, (b) they may or may not recur, and (c) you want to buy the property as cheaply as you can.

Thus, for starters, we are looking at a total rent of $103,500.

By the way, you will also note that some of the rents are ridiculously low. This is particularly true with respect to the Silver Stamp unit, which occupies the second largest space in the center. You will perceive with some relief that this lease expires in 1979, although you will not express this pleasurable emotion to the seller. Indeed, you will bemoan the short term remaining because it will make more difficult the job of finding some permanent financing (and it will). You

Tenant	Lease expires	Options	Annual rent	Overage percentage	Overage collected	Tax escalation	Square feet
Big Supermarket	7/31/91	3–5 yr	$ 34,000	1%		Yes	16,800
Beauty Shop	3/31/79	None	6,750	8%		Yes	2,250
Dry Cleaner	4/30/81	1–5 yr	6,750	7.5%		Yes	2,250
Silver Stamps	12/31/79	None	14,000	None		Yes	10,020
National Drug	8/31/81	None	12,000	2.5%	$7,000	No	7,650
Jeans	7/31/81	None	9,000	5%		Yes	2,700
Family Variety	12/31/86	2–3 yr	9,000	None		Yes	6,000
Delicatessen	2/28/80	1–5 yr	9,000	7%	6,000	Yes	2,250
Country Fried Chicken	5/30/79	1–5 yr	3,000	7%		Yes	1,215
		Total	$103,500				
		Overage	13,000				
			$116,500				

Taxes 1976	Insurance	Loan balance =	Monthly payments
$10,292.83	1,500	$289,947.20	$4,425 (6.75%)
		(at time of purchase)	

Figure 2

hope (assuming you are able to option the property at a reasonable price) that the lender will be sufficiently reassured by the grocery, variety, and drug-chain leases and will not hold the short-term stamp-store lease too strongly against you. At the expiration of that agreement (and you will note that the store has no renewal options) you will rent to another (or perhaps to the same) tenant at a minimum of $2 per square foot, thus increasing your base income by $6,040 per annum.

We have mentioned at an earlier time that permanent financing will not normally exceed 70 to 75 percent of the purchase price and that, in one way or another, the real estate commission—if one is involved—will be built into the purchase price.

In the actual case upon which our hypothetical is based, one of the investors was a real estate broker. You will see how this worked to our advantage in making arrangements for long-term financing.

Now let's add another qualifier. Our broker-investor learned of the possible availability of the property because the deceased partner-owner was a member of the former's church. After an appropriate interval, he made inquiry of one of the surviving partners, who in time came back with (a) the response that the project could be purchased and (b) the $825,000 tab.

The broker came to me with the proposition. He thought it looked good and that the price was negotiable. At the asking price, the return on total dollars involved was just over 12 percent, far too low.

We talked to our banker. He was familiar with the property, liked its location, agreed that at the right price it would be a proper investment, and said that he would be pleased to assist in the matter of arranging some financing.

From that point on, we proceeded through the

usual negotiation ritual, our colleague finally getting concurrence on a 120-day option at a purchase price of $700,000. At minimum rentals, this would not rate as the buy of the year, but remember those overages, which—though uncertain—would most likely recur. Remember, too, the strong possibility of re-leasing the stamp store at a minimum increase of $6,040.

If the overages just remained constant and the stamp-store unit could be leased in 1979 at $2 per foot, total rents would then come in at $122,540 for a gross return on purchase price of over 17.5 percent.

The price also means that for land and buildings you would only be paying $10 per square foot, whereas if you were building your own, construction costs alone would probably run 2 or 3 times that much. This comparison becomes relevant when one thinks in terms of future rents. Beyond any question, and in the not too distant future, this center will be renting at a substantially higher figure per square foot, if only because increased construction costs always tend to raise rents generally, even on older properties.

I mentioned earlier that our broker-associate had done the negotiating, and you may recall that in an earlier chapter I had suggested the advantages of having a real estate agent in your group and of letting him, or a lawyer colleague, handle all purchase negotiations.

In the actual case on which our hypothetical is based, we were able to improve our permanent financing position considerably. The permanent lender (which in this case turned out to be the mortgage loan division of our favorite bank) simply factored into the purchase price an amount sufficient to cover a reasonable commission—in this case 6 percent. Thus, for loan purposes, our purchase price was shown as $742,000. There was no deception practiced during this exercise. The broker's commission was $42,000, and whether we paid it or not was our business. The lender knew that the agent would be one of the owners. His own appraisal had indicated that we were getting a good buy, and he knew that if the seller was paying a commission, the purchase price would certainly have been raised sufficiently to cover it.

In round numbers, the loan commitment came through at $556,000, which represented a healthy 75 percent on $742,000 and which left us with only $144,000 of the purchase price to come up with from other sources.

Let's see what other cost items are going to be involved in consummating this particular purchase. For one thing, you are going to owe the loan-brokering agency a point (service fee of 1 percent, or $5,560 on your loan). In addition, there will be other closing costs—legal fees (the lawyer in your group will be disqualified from handling the work although he will most likely be able to get it done by other counsel at a discounted fee), title-insurance costs, survey costs, etc. Let's figure a total of $10,000 for everything.

All right. Including closing costs, you will have to come up with $154,000, a tidy figure.

Now let's look at some other expenses.

Let's say that your permanent commitment carries an interest rate of 9.75 percent and a term of twenty years, requiring an annual amortization of $63,285.25. We add to that current *ad valorem* taxes of $10,500 and insurance of $1,500. Utilities (which only involve exterior lighting) are currently running about $60 monthly, but we built in $1,200 per year for that item.

What about maintenance? Remember that here, as in all your projects, you have had the buildings carefully looked at, seeking particularly to find any evidence of structural decay. Your report on this property was highly affirmative on structural condition, though there are cosmetic needs which require attention pronto. You decide to budget $5,000 per year for maintenance.

Finally, you decide to put something in for rent loss due to vacancy and at 5 percent you eat up another— let's just make it a round number—$5,000, getting you up to $86,485.25 and leaving you a marginal $17,014.75 from your rent income of $103,500 for secondary financing.

Your work sheet now looks like this:

Purchase price	$700,000
Loan commitment	−556,000
	$144,000
Points and closing costs	10,000
Needed from other sources	$154,000

Annual expenses		Annual income	
Loan amortization	$63,285.25	Total rents	$103,500.00
Taxes	10,500.00	Expenses	−86,485.25
Insurance	1,500.00		$ 17,014.75
Utilities	1,200.00		
Maintenance	5,000.00		
Rent loss due to vacancy	5,000.00		
	$86,485.25		

Your commitment letter contains a prohibition against any secondary financing in which the property itself is used for security. Some lenders insist on this, others do not. In the case put, yours does. He doesn't want you to be too thin with your own commitment.

On the other hand, you need a little running room until you can get the project well under way, and besides, the idea of putting any consequential portion of your own funds into a project disturbs you mightily. In this situation, a short-term (say, two-year) unsecured loan might be indicated.

But remember that your income after expenses ($17,014.75) is based on no overages (highly improbable happening) and rents pegged at current (in some instances preposterously low) rentals. If, as we are projecting, you can get that rent total up to around $120,000 in a couple of years, then you'll have another $17,000 or so to play with, giving you close to $35,000 per year. Even in your first year, and even allowing for the proration of overages on which your seller insists, you should be able to increase that $17,000 to about $25,000, and thus, over a two-year period you can quite reasonably anticipate collecting $60,000 over and above expenses. If you're able to keep everything rented, your allowance for vacancy element can be added to this, giving you another $10,000.

Thus, on a reasonable balancing of the evidence, it would seem that you are in a position to assure substantial reduction in principal during the two-year loan period. Even with interest at, say, 8.5 percent, you could quite conceivably reduce principal by $50,000, leaving you with a $106,000 balance at the end of the two-year period.

By that time, your center should be functioning smoothly and you would be able to predict with more precision your net cash-flow position. In all probability your short-term lender (with whom you have been carrying the partnership account and who has thus been receiving the benefit of a so-called compensating balance) will not be displeased with your performance (particularly if you have made full disclosure of your plans in the first instance), but it—the lender—will most probably prefer that you either pay off the loan or else do some restructuring (e.g., break it out of the partnership structure and go on an individual basis).

What you and your partners decide to do in such a case will, in large measure, depend on your personal situations. Quite possibly you will have realized monies from the sale of some other asset, as, for example, of some raw land. You might want to reduce the principal by individual contributions to equity, thus reducing the loan balance by the amount of the contributions.

Remember that a purchase of this size is not the result of your initial foray into the real estate market. You should have other properties to lean on, and one of these could provide security (albeit second security) for another loan.

Finally, the original lender, given the fact that your compensating balance has been satisfactory, and particularly in a period of modest capital expansion generally, might be pleased to go another year with you under the original formula.

So long as your general financial statement is good, and the balance—in this instance, $106,000—is not of panic-inducing proportions when spread among the four of you, you need not be concerned. Project that the situation will arise when you acquire the property originally and start planning your next move well ahead of, in this case, the expiration of the two-year secondary-financing time line.

The important thing always is to keep the debt contained within the bounds of manageability. These boundaries should be determined by the financial limitations of the weakest person in your group and by the money-production potential of the property on which or for which you are borrowing.

Ten
Selling Raw Land

A banker friend of mine once made the observation that a lot of people know when to buy, but few know when to sell. This is a curious, but probably valid, comment. Just as people like to bet on winners, so they hate to let go of one. In the stock market, bulls make money and bears make money and hogs lose their assets, or so runs an ancient expression.

Sometimes it's a good idea to sell, but generally in the kinds of investment we've been discussing here, the opportunity will come to you rather than your seeking it. Our little groups have sold property, but we have never made an effort to do so.

Just as you will have searched for the property you ultimately acquire, so others will be searching and acquiring. Real estate experts for all kinds of land users are cruising constantly, spotting sites which will meet the needs of their clients, locating the owners, and negotiating for purchase.

In 1971, one of our groups purchased two adjoining parcels of real estate, one parcel giving frontage on a busy parkway around our city, the other adding depth to the first. Interestingly, the package was assembled by a broker who knew we were interested in acquiring land. He had shopped it extensively but without success until he came to us. Others contacted had felt the price on the front piece was too high (and it was). We viewed the two parcels as one (which once assembled they would become), and when total cost was spread over the entire tract (5 acres total) the per-foot cost was in line with values in the area.

More important, we were able to work out 10 percent down, ten-year financing on both properties. Both sellers were agreeable also to a release provision in the mortgages. You will recall our discussion of this very important point in the chapter dealing with acquisition of raw land. In this case—and this was a first and only for us, but it shows how totally flexible arrangements can be—we even were able to pay the broker on installments on the same schedule we paid the mortgages.

The agent had not been employed either by the sellers or by us. He had ingeniously seen the possibilities of joining the properties, and had received permission from the owners to contact potential buyers, but had no official listing status with either owner and, of course, no employment arrangement with us. It furnishes an example of a real estate fee well earned. But for the contact from the agent, we would never have known of or acquired this land or been able to enjoy the profits from its sale.

After acquiring the property, we held it until 1974, when we were approached by a seller of motor homes who wanted to acquire land for his sales center. We sold him a portion of the property at 4 times what we had paid for it (based on an average of our purchase prices on the two original parcels). The next year we sold an additional section of the property to a fast-food franchisee who preferred owning his own land at 5 times its cost to us.

Then along came a mini-warehouse developer who wanted a small piece of frontage and a lot of acreage. Here, the added depth we'd acquired would come in handy. Again, the contact was made by a broker who knew of our property and who also knew the warehouse people were searching for sites in several cities, ours among them.

The broker, for whose services we ultimately paid, contacted us with a proposition from the proposed buyer. It was not satisfactory, and it read essentially as follows:

Seller would option the property, based on a $100,000 purchase price, for $1,000. The option money would be refunded if after twenty days seller decided it could not use the land for the purpose desired. If seller did not within the 20-day period request return of the money, seller would have an additional 120 days coverage for its $1,000 investment and an additional 30 days for closing if it exercised the option. We would pay $10,000 brokerage.

Apart from the dubious legal validity of the proposal (stemming from the right to reclaim the $1,000 after twenty days), the offer was simply unacceptable. We countered with the following terms:

The option price would be $2,500, which would be available for immediate distribution to our partners but returnable, of course, if buyer ultimately exercised the option and we could not convey clear title. There would be no right of refund after twenty days and the option would extend for a total of sixty days with fifteen additional days for closing. The price would be $100,000 *exclusive* of brokerage.

We did not back off from this counteroffer, and buyer, after much protesting, finally agreed to it (we allowed him fifteen days to accept or reject our proposition).

You might take note of our request for the right to disburse the $2,500 immediately. Rules of ethics for real estate agents often provide that monies paid to them as good-faith deposits must be held in the agent's trust account until such time as the transaction is concluded by purchase of the property or forfeiture of the deposit. If, however, the parties agree to the contrary, the agent is not bound by this stricture and may disburse the funds to the seller.

The reason for the rule is obvious. If buyer elected to purchase and seller could not convey good title, then buyer would be entitled to the return of his deposit and the money should be immediately available to him in such cases, as it obviously would be if it were in the broker's trust account.

Here, of course, we knew our title was clear. As I mentioned in the beginning, you should always have title certified before acquiring property. It was obvious we could put the option money to better use than would be the case if it rested in the broker's trust account.

In the case put, buyer ultimately (on the fifty-ninth day of the sixty days of option) advised us in writing—and by telephone—that the option would be exercised, and it was, and everyone, at least up to this writing, has lived happily afterward, including the broker, who by putting buyer and seller together, picked up a cool $10,000.

Sometimes in selling, again in cases where raw land is involved, you will be confronted with a request for personal financing. You are then on the other side of the equation we discussed in Chapter 5, where you were the buyer. Here you will just have to let your financial situation be your guide. If the price is right, time financing can be a good thing. You are getting interest on the deferred payment; you are probably getting a great deal more for your land than you paid for it; and if need for instant cash arises, you can always take your note for the balance to the bank and have it discounted, i.e., sell the paper for its present value—less the interest it would have earned, of course, and minus a factor (or price, if you will) for having money owed to you in the future paid to you now. There are times when discounting paper in this manner will be a helpful ploy for you, as where you run into a buy opportunity which you think is unusually good and you need some quick and otherwise unavailable cash to take advantage of it. Obviously, your prime consideration here will be whether the projected appreciation in value of the property you propose to purchase will outstrip the amount you would receive in interest if you hold on to your note and mortgage.

I once heard a wise woman remark that when opportunity knocked on her door, she didn't want to mistake its summons for that of a neighbor. When opportunity knocks in real estate, it's great if you are in a position to take advantage of the summons, even if you have to sacrifice some immediate economic advantage to do so.

Eleven
Selling Income Property

Just as considerations in buying income-producing property differ from those involved in buying raw land, so there are differences when sale time comes.

If you are under no compulsion to sell, you can objectively impose standards which will ensure that you receive an adequate price. What is an adequate price?

Well, obviously, it should be more than you paid for the property, although to this, as to all rules—especially obvious ones—there are exceptions. You might, for example, sense a changing of the neighborhood where your property is located and feel that in the long run the change will not improve property values. You may have already received enough benefits from the property in tax savings through shelter (and in positive cash-flow benefits if your shelter has run out or the rental income has, through overages or for other reasons, been exceptionally high).

Just as in buying you should set a ceiling on the price you'll pay, so in selling you should set a floor on the price for which you'll sell. You know that most buyers will want a decent return on their investment, and generally in selling you should make your calculations on the basis of total sales price rather than buyer's cash-on-cash return (in most instances you won't even know what that will be). If it's commercial property and overages are involved, make as much of that as you possibly can. You'll remember that from the buyer's side you need to minimize overages on the perfectly logical ground that the only really reliable income indicator is the fixed rental. On the seller's side, and particularly if the overage pattern is well and predictably established, you should contend that the percentage return has so stabilized as to suggest it will continue, at least at its present level.

The buyer is going to want to buy at a price which will yield him 18 to 20 percent, and you should try to hold his return to 12 or 14 percent. These figures, generally speaking, provide the framing in today's market and—absent some dramatic decrease or increase in interest rates—will foreseeably continue to do so.

But again remember that we are not pricing stocks and bonds or diamonds. We are pricing a commodity which has no precisely measurable market factors on either the buy or sell side. Subjective personal considerations will often count for more than objective economic ones in arriving at a sales price for real estate.

Suppose, for example, that the property you're selling is that office building and that the potential purchasers are a couple of dentists or doctors who just happen to want a building of that size in that general location for their own use. Obviously, they will be interested not so much in the potential yield on their investment but in how the building will serve their practice, how it will feel as a more or less permanent "home."

Or again, suppose that your potential buyer is desperately in search of some shelter and would, paradoxically, be better off paying more than less. He, or his agent, will hardly put himself in the position of asking you to raise the price, but some knowledge on your part of his situation will materially assist you in your sales negotiations.

It is just as important to make an independent investigation of your buyer's situation as it is for your seller's when you're on the other side of the fence. If you're dealing with a broker and he is reluctant to identify his principal (client), insist that he do so. Tell him you must know with who you're dealing; that if you sell the property, you will want it to be to a buyer who will treat it as reverentially as you have.

Remember, if you're selling and you're not under compulsion, you have all the leverage. Remember, too, that there are no price controls or standards to restrict or inhibit you.

In a given situation, you might quote one price for cash, another if seller wants you to finance a portion of his total costs. In the latter case, you might counter with an agreement to finance—either as prime lender or with the security of a second mortgage—but only if you receive a higher sales price. Deferred income, after all, is not worth as much as present income (except where an installment sale might be better for you from a capital gains standpoint, but that is a personal matter and should have no bearing on your dealings with any buyer). Buyer will often pay the higher price.

Second mortgages, of course, are not as desirable as first ones, but if you're getting enough money and have confidence in the buyer and the property, it is perfectly appropriate, and often good business, to take a second note and mortgage.

In all sales, whether of raw land or improved property, you will need to look at your income-tax consequence.

Twelve
Condemnation

We have mentioned the possibility of your property being taken by the government or other authorized agencies (e.g., public utility) under the power of eminent domain.

You should anticipate such sovereign action in any commercial lease agreement. Apartment leases are normally short-term (rarely more than a year) and seldom present a problem in condemnation cases as between landlord and tenant. Leases of business property are another breed of cat.

Absent some contrary provision in the lease agreement, the lessee shares in the condemnation award. To what extent is a question shrouded in fog. The theory supporting lessee's participation is based, of course, on his right to control the land during the period of his lease and indeed through the time granted by any renewal options. The measure of such leasehold value is generally said to be the difference between the fair and reasonable value of the unexpired portion of the lease and the rent actually reserved by the lease. If lessee can't go elsewhere and rent in a comparable location, for a comparable price, for a similar time period—and if his lease has several years to run—then he has something of substantial value. If the parties can't agree as to what this value really is, then the court in a condemnation proceeding must decide it, and that is not always an easy task.

Many courts hold that in no event shall the total award exceed the fair market value of the real estate itself. Sometimes, the proceeding is bifurcated. The awarding authority (court-appointed referee or commissioners or jury of one's peers) is instructed to decide upon the value of the real estate, then, in a second proceeding, to decide on a measure of division between the parties.

At the very least, lessee would normally receive the difference between the rent he's paying his landlord and the rent he will now have to pay someone else. If there has been a mite of inflation since the original lease was drawn, the amount could be substantial.

But—aha!—there is a way to avoid the problem. Build some anticipatory language into the lease in the first instance. "In the event any or all of the demised property is condemned during the period of this lease, in such manner as to render it unusable for the conduct of lessee's business, then either party may terminate this agreement. Lessee shall not be entitled to share in any award of money for such taking, whether received through settlement or paid under court order." Obviously, the lessee does not have to agree to this, but I've yet to find one who refused to. Rarely do leases contain such language, and plenteous are the cases involving settlements between lessor and lessee.

In most instances, the result is not as harsh for the lessee as might at first blush appear. Most agencies (and all of them using federal funds in whole or in part) are committed to the Uniform Relocation Act, which provides comforting benefits to the displaced tenant, including moving expenses, help in finding new quarters, and a displacement allowance. (All of this assistance is in addition to the condemnation award.)

But even though you have anticipated—and by appropriate wording in your lease avoided—a possible disagreement between you and your rentee, what about the more basic question of *your* rights against the condemnor?

Condemnation proceedings are always preceded by a letter from the taker, advising that your property has become an impediment to public progress and suggesting that a representative of condemnor will call and advise you of your rights. He will call in due course and he will advise you and he will probably tell you what he is authorized to pay. The Constitution provides that he must pay "just compensation" when taking "private property for public use."

"Just compensation" to the negotiator will mean all or most of what the government appraisers have said your property is worth. Government appraisers (private citizens, normally, who are skilled in real estate appraisal and are hired as independent contractors to value properties in a given project) are not always wrong, but neither are they always right.

Usually, the price offered is a synthesis of two or three appraisals, in fact, and between these there may have been considerable differential. Some agencies decree that if there is more than a 20-percent difference between the first two appraisals, then a third must be obtained, and somewhere between the figures each of these skilled professionals develops must—the government reasons—lie the truth.

You might think otherwise, as the Constitution gives you every right to do, and go in quest of your own skilled professional appraisers. These stout fellows, spurred by your invitation, might study your property and conclude that the government valuation is ridiculously low and that instead of being worth, say, $50,000, as the government appraisal would suggest, your land in fact has a fair market value ("the price a willing buyer would pay to a willing seller, neither being under compulsion") of $100,000.

In such event, you should most certainly request a hearing on the question of value. You would find, I suspect, as property owners have been discovering for years, that the hearing agency tends to wind up somewhere in between government and property-owner valuations—say, in your case, somewhere around $80,000.

Traditionally, lawyers have represented landowners in condemnation cases on a contingent fee basis— a percentage of any amount they were able to obtain over and above the amount offered to you before you sought help of counsel.

In recent years, more and more states and localities have enacted laws providing for payment of the property owner's counsel fees by the condemnor in an amount to be set by the court. The rationale of this perfectly reasonable fringe benefit is that the constitutional "just compensation" for property taken in this fashion means what it says and that an aggrieved property owner should not have his judicially determined "just compensation" diminished by the lawyer's extraction therefrom.

Sometimes the condemnation involves the preemption of an easement (the right of another to use your property for certain purposes but with title remaining in your name). Indeed, this is almost always the case where utility companies (which generally have the power of eminent domain to facilitate the installation of power and transmission lines) are the moving parties and sometimes (though with ever-lessening frequency) where the state or one of its agencies is seeking additional road right-of-way

Don't be deceived by the term "easement." Just as a rose by any name hath a rosy smell, a taking by any name is a taking. One power company with which we have had frequent dealings makes a habit of employing kindly, courtly old gentlemen to negotiate easement rights for the installation of its power-transmitting facilities. Once the company has decided what should be the proper routing for its new addition (and it is almost impossible to veto the choice), these minions are sent out in search of owners of the affected properties. They perform magnificently.

In one case handled by my office (the numbers have been changed slightly, but the differentials have not), the client—who owned 240 acres of land in a fast-developing suburban section—was advised that the line would require 150 feet of right-of-way width across his entire tract, the whole easement covering approximately 20 acres. The kindly, courtly negotiator offered $7,000 for this taking, reminding our client that he could still cultivate the ground beneath the power lines and even (with the consent and approval of the company) put roadways under them. Our man did not feel that the dollars offered were sufficient, particularly when he looked at power lines in place and observed that they affected not only the ground directly under them but also had a spillover value detriment to lands outside their precise path.

He requested that we represent him. We contacted the power company and within a short time were advised that they had reviewed their original offer and supporting appraisals and had concluded that the fair value of the easement required was $36,000.

This response, gratifying though it was, did not titillate our client, who requested that we let the court decide. The court did so, concluding that the power company was wrong both times and that the damage done to the property was in fact $80,000. Later we learned that there were 160 separately owned tracts in the right-of-way and that the company's negotiators had acquired 157 easements on their own terms. Let's just call it shocking.

In another case we recently handled, the daughter of a landowner in Piedmont, North Carolina, came to us with a terribly sad story. The mother-owner was elderly and in poor health. The daughter had negotiated in her mother's behalf the sale of a portion of that woman's 100-acre land tract to an industrial user. The land was well located, near a major airfield and with superior highway and rail access. The only problem was that when the prospective purchaser's lawyer started looking at the chain of title, he discovered that twenty years earlier the mother had signed a right-of-way agreement in favor of a large pipeline company. This astonishing document provided for a pittance payment for the installation of the first line and gave the company the right to install as many lines as it desired at any future time on payment of a nominal sum per lineal rod. The lawyer correctly advised his client that the land was useless, since at any moment and forever the company could come in and lay another pipeline.

We brought a court action to reform the instrument, contending that it was indecent; that its execution had been obtained under unsportsmanlike conditions; and, more important, that it constituted an invalid restraint on alienation and violated an ancient rule of property law called the Rule Against Perpetuities. None of these arguments got us to first base, and, of course, we had to get there if we were to score at all.

Then one of the young brains in my office came up with an ingenious conception, premised on the ancient legal rule of interpretation that ambiguities in written documents will be resolved against the party who drew the paper in the first place. In our case, of course, this was the pipeline company.

The document, my young associate pointed out, *did not specify whether the pipes were to be laid horizontally or vertically!* An elderly farm woman in North Carolina might have assumed that they were to be laid vertically, thus preserving the land to either side of the original path for her heirs, successors, and assigns to do with as they chose.

I wish I could tell you that we won the case on this lovely point. In fact, we did not prevail, but we did make enough impression on the corporation's counsel to obtain a settlement under the terms of which the company agreed to limit its right of incursion.

In sum, don't sign anything without a lawyer's approval, and not just any lawyer's. Condemnation law is a specialized field and getting rapidly more so. Seek and ye shall find a barrister who does this sort of thing often and well.

Thirteen
Going It Alone

Let's suppose that, however interesting the group investment concept is to you, it just won't work in your case. Your business or your social situation is such that you are not thrown together with or haven't become acquainted with other folk who might be disposed to join in the kind of partnership venture I've outlined.

There is no law, of course, against going it alone, or in partnership with your spouse.

Maybe you've been stashing your own overage, if any, after meeting the obligations of living, in a savings account or perhaps in some stocks. Almost any amount is sufficient to get you started in the real estate business.

Let's put a case. You have $10,000 invested—$5,000 of it in a stock you like and $5,000 in a mutual fund.

Both—the mutual, particularly—have been spectacularly unimpressive in performance, but you feel a certain allegiance to the stock. It's always good to have some ready liquidity anyway, so you decide to put that portion of your portfolio represented by the mutual investment into real estate, saving the stock for what you hope will be some growth and because in any event it will give you some quick liquidity.

You then start casting about for a piece of real estate.

Except for the dollars involved, everything we have said in the preceding chapters can apply to your personal investment program. You could, for instance, decide to put this money into raw land, speculating on appreciation. On the other hand, you might want to get some personal tax benefit from income-producing property, as well as the automatic equity buildup that goes with it. You opt for the latter.

You start looking at the real estate section of your favorite newspaper. You lean toward a small business property but realize that with no more front money than $5,000 it would have to be small indeed. You also think in terms of a duplex apartment, figuring that if worse comes to worst, you can always live in one half of it.

You recognize, in the absence of any secondary borrowing, that your money will probably get you a property costing about $20,000. With secondary borrowing, you can leverage that up somewhat, maybe by $5,000 or $10,000.

You respond to a number of advertisements and look at several properties. They are either too expensive or too cheap. You are not interested in slum or slum-prone real estate holdings.

Then one day you receive a call from an agent with whom you'd had earlier conversation. He has listed a small property in a suburban location which might interest you. It is a 100- by 300-foot lot, presently occupied by an old single-story home which is and has been for some years used as a beauty parlor. The property is zoned for business, and there is ample room behind the house for another building. The asking price is $50,000, but the owner will finance a good portion of that. The beauty shop operator has been there five years and is in the first year of a new three-year lease. She has an excellent business, and the building, though elderly, is in good repair. The tenant pays $400 per month against a 7-percent overage and last year paid a total of $5,200. The owner pays the taxes ($600) and insurance ($150), but there is a tax escalation clause in the new lease and the operator has just added two additional chairs because of recent growth in her business.

The owner of the building has recently retired and is moving out of state to live with his daughter and her family. He wants to sell all of his local holdings. Maybe this one is for you.

You drive by the property and are pleased with what you see. It *is* an old house but has obviously been well cared for. It sits on a level, grassed lot, maybe 20 feet from the sidewalk. "The lot alone is worth the asking price," the agent says. The lot is once removed from the corner, and on the corner lot sits a service station of modern design. On the other side of the house is an old single-story office building occupied by an automobile finance company. Surrounding residential properties are older, but well kept. An elementary school is located in the next block.

What have you got to lose? The tenant seems durable enough. To be sure, she might go out of business tomorrow, but her history argues against that. She has demonstrated sufficient optimism to commit herself to a new three-year lease, a tax escalation clause, and perhaps most revealingly, *two additional chairs.* Last year she paid $5,200 under a 7-percent overage formula, indicating a gross of almost $75,000. With the new facilities she will most likely up that by more than a smattering—say, to $85,000, which would see your gross rental edging its way up to $6,000.

On last year's $5,200, you obviously aren't doing sensationally—just over 9 percent on total cost of property. At $6,000, you'd be getting 12 percent. Remember, too, that there's additional room on the property to either (a) expand the existing structure or (b) build another one. What would the cash on cash look like?

Before we know what cash on cash will look like, we have to strike a bargain. You have $5,000, the asking price is $50,000, and the owner, as the expression is, will take some paper. Remember, direct financing with the owner is, in most cases, the finest financing of all. You try for the best and ask the agent to transmit an offer of $5,000 cash, balance in ten years, payable in equal annual installments of principal and interest, the latter at the rate of 7 percent per annum. The agent tells you that it would be useless to submit such an offer, but you insist that he do so anyway. He does and shortly comes back with a report.

It was useless to submit such an offer, he reports.

You then tell the agent you'd like to have a savings and loan institution look at the property for loan-evaluation purposes, that you are definitely interested, and that you hope he won't let the property get away until you've had an opportunity to get this done. He pledges his cooperation to the extent possible ("Somebody might come along and offer the old boy $50,000 cash while you're fooling around, but I'll do what I can.").

In the matter of institutional borrowing, be advised that whenever and wherever possible it's best to work with local concerns, preferably a savings and loan. The loans are generally less cumbersome in terms of accompanying paperwork requirements, and you can almost always get a quick answer on your application. In the hypothetical with which we are now concerned, in fact, your local savings and loan would be quite possibly the *only* source of funds you'd have anyway.

In most cases, these institutions give priority to residential loans, and the availability of money for the type of borrowing you're contemplating will vary from time to time and from bank to bank. If money for such loans is available, you simply make application, pay a modest appraisal fee (prospective loan properties are normally appraised by an appraisal committee within a few days after application is made), and wait for the result.

In the current situation, you might have been well advised to try for an option pending the outcome of your application ($50,000 conditioned on being able to get a loan of at least $30,000, with owner to take second paper of $15,000). That is a judgment the agent can assist you in making. If he has confidence in his ability to control the situation, and you have confidence in the agent, you probably are not taking too much of a chance to proceed without option protection. In a few days, you get your answer.

Let me insert parenthetically, and before telling you what the answer is, that appraisers in such instances will rarely put a higher value than the proposed purchase price on any property, and you will always be asked to state in your loan application the amount you plan to pay for the property. You will recall that we have spoken earlier of the possible advantages of (a) actually owning the property when you apply for a loan and (b) having a real estate agent on your team so that his fee—whether or not you plan to pay it—can be built into the price.

All right. Now for your answer. Appraisal: $50,000 (What did I tell you? At least it wasn't less). Approved loan: $30,000. Interest rate: 9 percent. Term: twenty years. Monthly payments of principal and interest: $269.92, for a total annual outgo of $3,239.04.

Add in taxes ($600, locked in, remember, because of the escalation clause in the new lease) and insurance ($150) and we're up to $3,989.04 in annual payout, with $20,000 of principal still to be accounted for.

We have $5,000 cash (from the mutual sale), so that gets the remainder down to $15,000.

Now we go back to Roger Realtor. We could waste some more time trying to get a lower purchase price and might succeed, but let's assume we don't do either (waste more time or get a lower price). We tell Roger we'll pay $35,000 at the front and give a second paper, secured with a second mortage, for $15,000, payable in ten annual equal installments of principal and interest, the latter at the rate of 7 percent. We ask for the right of prepayment without penalty. We also—and here's the kicker—build into our offer another provision: The ten annual installments obligation does not begin for two years. In the interim, you will pay only interest—7 percent on $15,000, or $1,050 per annum—with the right to accelerate the schedule at your option.

If seller accepts, you are then committed to $5,039.04 for each of the first two years (forgetting for the moment any maintenance problems; these should be negligible anyway. The lease provides that tenant maintains the interior of the structure, and all the brick exterior needs is an occasional painting of the trim and you only need do some mowing of the grass in the rear of the property).

For ease of calculation, let's make the not unrealistically optimistic assumption that your rent in the first year is $6,039.04. Forgetting closing costs (which would probably run you from $300 to $400), your immediate cash-on-cash return would be 20 percent, *but* in two years you would have to start biting off that principal.

Apropos of this future commitment, I venture these thoughts. First, you have the doctrine of ALOTCHITY ("A lot of things can happen in two years") to rely on. The holder of the second paper may want to discount it. Your tenant may find her business booming to such an extent that she is not only paying considerably more rent but needs additional space as well. You will presumably be continuing in your own employment and perhaps bettering your income from that source. Second, you can take the $1,000 or so remaining after amortization and expenses and deposit it in savings against the day you'll have to start paying on principal. After all, you won't owe that first payment of principal for *three* years, and within that period you will have been able to save (by reason of no principal-payment requirements) almost $3,000 (plus a modicum of interest).

You rejoice when Roger Realtor reports back that the seller has accepted your proposition, and in due course you close the transaction on this basis.

You have started. For $5,000 (plus closing costs) you've acquired an income-producing property valued at $50,000. All you have to do now is enjoy owning your first investment property, collect the rents, pay the bills, and look to the future—when, as surely as the tides roll in and out, your holding will continue to increase in value and yield while your cost remains forever the same.

Fourteen
Tax Consequences

Every capital transaction these days has to be thought of in terms of tax consequences. When you buy or when you sell you're having an impact on the financing mechanism of the United States government, as well as, most likely, the fiscal affairs of the state in which you live. It is not enough to know that you bought for one dollar and are selling for two. You must also know how the sale will affect you—as the expression is—taxwise.

We start with some rather fundamental principles. Let's keep it simple and assume that you have acquired your property the hard way, that is, by purchase as opposed to by gift or inheritance.

Gains and Losses

What you paid for it becomes what, in tax parlance, is known as your basis. Everything that happens thereafter is keyed to that. Neither rain nor sleet nor snow nor the ravages of time will change your basis. If you hold your property for at least a year, any subsequent sale at a price higher than your cost price will result in what is known as a long-term capital gain. Any profitable sale within a shorter period is called—you guessed it—a short-term capital gain. The same distinction applies to capital losses.

Both kinds of capital gains can be offset against both kinds of capital losses. All capital gains are taxed (short-term at ordinary income rates, long-term at a percentage of the gain), but not all capital losses are deductible. If you have no offsetting gains, or if your losses exceed your gains substantially, you may offset only a limited amount of loss against ordinary income. As of this writing, if your capital loss is short-term, you get dollar for dollar but only up to $3,000 (it was limited to $1,000 until 1977, then moved to $2,000 for that year, and finally for 1978 and the foreseeable future, to the record-breaking $3,000 plateau). If your capital loss is long-term, you offset on a 50-percent basis, e.g., $6,000 of loss will only wash out $3,000 of ordinary income.

As an illustration, if you pay $100,000 for your property and hold it for more than one year, then sell it for $200,000, you are taxed a percentage (up to 35 percent) of the $100,000 gain.

On the other hand, if you pay $200,000, hold it for more than a year, and sell it for $100,000, you may not take all or even 35 percent of the difference as a loss. You are limited to $3,000 of naked loss (or excess of loss over gain) in any one year. In the case put, since the loss was long-term, it would require $6,000 of it to get that $3,000 offset.

The other side of the coin is that you can carry this healthy loss forward for an unlimited time and offset it against any gains you might have in that period.

Involuntary Conversion

Sometimes you have to sell whether you want to or not. We have warned you against letting yourself get into this fix insofar as you have any control over your situation, but sometimes the state wrests this control away from you in the exercise of what is referred to as the right of eminent domain, i.e., the power to take private property for public use.

Of course, in such circumstances, the law provides that the affected property owner must be fairly compensated.

For tax purposes, a taking, by constituted governmental authority or private utilities having the power of eminent domain, either by or under the threat of legal condemnation, makes your property the subject of an "involuntary conversion" (the same effects flow from destruction of property by forces beyond your control, e.g., by fire, if monies are received by you—as from insurance—in consequence thereof and in reimbursement for your loss). Gains and losses are recognized in such instances, but the immediate sale is tax-free *if* the property owner reinvests the proceeds in similar property. As to real property converted after October 4, 1976, the taxpayer now has three years *following* the end of the tax year in which the taking occurred within which to perform the reinvestment ceremony. The newly acquired land has the same basis as the converted property. Adjustments are made up or down if what is subsequently purchased costs more or less than the amount realized from the involuntary sale.

Swaps

In addition to selling property—voluntarily or involuntarily—one can exchange it, and the exchange will be tax-free to the extent of its overlapping. If there's any difference on either side, adjustment is made accordingly.

A variant of the direct swap is what is sometimes referred to as the "tradearound." Let's say you want to buy the Love Apartments. You ask the owners if they'll sell. They say no, but they'll trade for the Beech Apartments, which they've been advised are for sale. The Beech property is of comparable age, size, and condition. You learn that the Beech Apartments are for sale, so just like that you buy them and exchange your new holding for the Love place. Assuming it's an even swap, the Love people pay no tax and you own the property you wanted in the first place. When later you sell, your basis will of course be what you paid for the Beech building.

Depreciation

Earlier we've explained what depreciation is. Now let's look at some of its mechanics.

The Internal Revenue Code allows an annual depreciation deduction based on a reasonable allowance for wear and tear (including—and this sometimes becomes particularly important in real estate—obsolescence) of business and income-producing property.

The depreciation allowance is vital for the regeneration of capital, and every red-blooded citizen should be continuously *en garde* against any congressional effort to erode it. Depreciation is not to be confused with depletion. The former deals with replaceable assets, while the latter applies to ever-diminishing and irreplaceable supplies in nature.

Land as such may not be depreciated for the simple reason that it is not going anywhere and is not wearing out, either. It doesn't matter what ravages time or pollution or a neighboring owner have wrought. Land—in the eyes of the law, anyway—cannot be worn and torn. Improvements on land (e.g., buildings) are depreciable. How rapidly and in what manner depends on a number of factors, some of which we will mention. But all calculations of depreciation are based on the estimated remaining life of the property.

How Do You Determine This Sort of Life Expectancy?   Unfortunately, there are no mortuary tables for buildings as there are for people. The obliging IRS, however, has jumped into that breach and come up with guidelines to aid you in determining the probable life span of various kinds of structures. In keeping with its accustomed practices, the Service cheerfully makes these projections available to you. If I were in your place, I would cheerfully accept them at face value or else come up with some awfully good evidence as to why they shouldn't apply.

How Do You Determine the Dollars Involved?   Well, this was determined for you when you bought the property to be depreciated. Your cost is what you depreciate, and, obviously, since the land itself is not depreciable, you must separate the cost of buildings from the cost of land. Normally no breakdown is set out in a contract of purchase, and even if the parties agreed on one and put it in the contract, it wouldn't be binding on the IRS. Reasonable judgment is called for in these cases.

How Do You Make a Reasonable Judgment?

1.   You may rely on your own judgment, of course. Let's say the property involved is your two-building apartment complex. Ask a friend in the real estate business what land zoned for multi-family dwellings is selling for in that neighborhood and relate that to the amount of land in your project, then subtract the dollars from your purchase price.

Check the local tax records. They will show a breakdown between land and improvements, not binding on anyone but the local tax collector, to be sure, but nonetheless offering a reasonably educated backup opinion to your own.

2.   Solicit your accountant's judgment. His may be the best advice you can come by.

3.   If all else fails, or if for some reason the valuation in your particular case is unusually complex, call in an appraiser. Get one who belongs to the Master Appraisal Institute or the Society of Real Estate Appraisers. These individuals wear their MAI or SRA credentials as proudly as a medic wears his M.D. and for almost as good a reason. They have worked and studied over long periods to gain admission to these elite appraisal bodies. Any community will also have competent people whose appraisal techniques are highly regarded by lenders and other users in the area, but who for their own reasons have not sought special, nationally acknowledged professional status. Any savings and loan officer can give you their names. Tell your ultimate choice you simply want a percentage allocation of value—e.g., 75 percent building, 25 per-

cent land, and try to get his price in advance. Of course, you will want his opinion in writing.

One hears complaints on occasion that the depreciation formula is unfair in that it does not (as do conventional expenses) reflect the impact of inflation. The depreciation deduction is always based on dollar values at the time of acquisition. One does not hear complaints of this nature, I would wager, in a deflationary period, but of course (at least so far as real estate is concerned) we rarely experience those anyway.

There are two types of depreciation schedules: (1) *straight-line* (the kind with which you'll generally be concerned) and (2) *accelerated*. In both, you are taking the dollars involved and spreading them over the estimated remaining life of the property. If a building has an estimated remaining life of twenty years, the basic working factor for depreciation is 1/20, or 5 percent per year.

Straight-line Depreciation   Straight-line depreciation may be used for any property. You simply depreciate the basic percentage of the building's value each year. If your building is worth $20,000 with an estimated life of twenty years, your yearly depreciation would be 5 percent of $20,000, or $1,000.

Accelerated Depreciation   Primarily, you accelerate by one of two methods: (1) declining balance and (2) sum of the digits.

In the former mode, you can depreciate (depending on the situation) at the rate of 200 percent, 150 percent, or 125 percent of the basic factor. In our example above, under the 200-percent formula, the basic factor of 1/20 (5 percent) becomes 2/20 (10 percent). However, the amount is not constant as in straight-line depreciation but is recalculated every year on the balance remaining after the previous year's depreciation has been subtracted.

The 200-percent method is limited to new residential property where at least 80 percent of the gross rental comes from dwelling units. The 150-percent or 125-percent declining-balance computation may be used for any new real estate (you're the first owner), and 125 percent may also be employed for used residential properties if at the time of acquisition by you they have a remaining useful life of twenty or more years.

Let's look at some examples of these, taking always a valuation of $20,000 and a useful life of twenty years. Under straight-line depreciation, we would simply deduct 5 percent (20 into 100), or $1,000, per annum.

If we were dealing with new residential, using the 200-percent method, we would use a factor of 10 percent (2 times 5 percent) so that in the first year our deduction would be $2,000. The second year, we would apply the 10 percent to the remaining depreciable amount ($18,000) and come out with $1,800. The third year our figure would be one-tenth of $16,200—and so on. As you can readily see, your depreciation benefit is heavy at the front but will tail rapidly in the later portion of your twenty-year span.

The 150-percent method works on the same principle, of course, your factor becoming 7.5 percent (1½ times 5 percent) instead of 10 and your first year's deduction $1,500 instead of $2,000. In the second year you would take 7.5 percent of $18,500, or $1,387.50, and beyond that the subtraction gets slightly more complicated.

At 125 percent, you would be working with 6.25 percent, $1,250 in the first year as opposed to straight line's $1,000.

Sum of the digits—available, remember, only for

new residential—is another fractional story. To get the applicable formula, you multiply the basis of the property by a fraction consisting of the remaining years of the depreciation period at the beginning of the taxable year over the sum of the digits for each of the years in the total depreciation period.

$$\frac{\text{Remaining years of depreciation period}}{\substack{\text{Sum of digits of years in} \\ \text{total depreciation period,} \\ \text{i.e., } 1 + 2 + 3 \ldots + 20}} \times \text{basis} = \text{depreciation}$$

In our case, then (twenty-year remaining life), the sum of the digits for one through twenty is 210. Thus the first year's depreciation is 20/210 of $20,000, or $1,904.76, somewhat heavier than we came up with using 200-percent declining.

$$\frac{20}{210} \times \$20,000 = \$1,904.76$$

You won't be concerned with sum of the digits because you'll be buying *used* apartments—if, that is, you've agreed with my earlier suggestions.

You can always change in midstream from an accelerated to a straight-line formula but not vice versa.

What Happens When You Sell   When you sell your property you have to give back—in one form and sometimes another—the depreciation you've taken.

If you've been straight line, then your basis is reduced by the amount of depreciation reserved. Let's take our $20,000 figure, for example, and say that the total original cost to you was $23,500. You allocated $20,000 to the improvements ($3,500 to land) and at the time of sale had depreciated for three years—$1,000 per annum—a total of $3,000.

Thus, your basis has become $20,500. If your sales price is, say, $30,000, your gains tax would be computed on $9,500 of profit rather than the $6,500 differential between selling price and original purchase price. The rationale for this is obvious. The government has permitted you to get back $3,000 of your original investment tax-free so that in net effect you had only paid $20,500. It did that on the assumption you would rebuild your building after it had worn out. Obviously you decided against that course, so to avoid a freeloader stigma you have to give the money back in this fashion.

If you had been under an accelerated formula, the government would have *recaptured* the amount by which acceleration permitted you to exceed straight-line depreciation. That excess would be taxed as ordinary income.

For example, let's suppose—using the same figures—you were using 150-percent declining and sold after three years. In that period, you would have depreciated a total of $4,191.87 ($1,500 plus $1,387.50 plus $1,284.37), $1,191.87 over straight line's $3,000. Your basis would still be $20,500 and you would pay a capital gains tax on $9,500. To that would be added a tax on the $1,191.87 excess at ordinary income rates.

Suggestion: Even in that rare case where you could use acceleration (the franchise building) think twice before you speed it up. If you intend to keep the property for the foreseeable future, my advice would be to play it straight.

There are other niceties in depreciation. You can break your building into its components—carpeting, air conditioning, plumbing—and depreciate these separately and rapidly. On the other hand, by not breaking them out in this naked fashion, you may permissibly shorten the overall projection of useful life on the entire structure. Let your accountant assist your judgment on this, as in all transactions impinging on the federal taxing law. The way things are now, not many don't.

Installment Sales

We have spoken earlier of the advantages of installment selling. If you do not realize more than 30 percent of the sales price in the year of the sale, *and* the remaining payments are spread over more than one calendar year, you may then spread the amount of the gain (and thus your tax on it) over the period of the installment payments. In such instances, you will apply, each year, the percentage of contract price which the gain represents to that particular year's installment.

Let's look at some examples:

1. Suppose A sells property having a basis of $120,000 for $200,000, payable $60,000 in cash and $140,000 in three annual installments of $40,000 and one final payment of $20,000. A's profit, obviously, is $80,000. So, 40 percent ($80,000 profit divided by $200,000 sales price) of each payment is recognized gain.

Thus, the projection will look about like this: On the down payment of $60,000, the gain is $24,000. On the next three payments the gain is $16,000 (40 percent of $40,000), and on the final $20,000 installment the gain is $8,000, all adding up to $80,000, on which total, but for his installment-sale procedure, A would have had to pay the full tax in the year of sale.

2. Suppose there had been a mortgage on the property. We'll postulate the same sale numbers as before—$200,000 sale, $120,000 basis, and $60,000 cash at the front—but here we have the complicating factor of a first mortgage in the amount of $40,000 to be assumed by buyer. Buyer will give seller a note and

second mortgage in the amount of $100,000, payable in five annual installments of $20,000.

A's profit is $80,000, to be accounted for as the money is paid in. Therefore, 50 percent ($80,000 profit divided by $160,000 contract price) of each payment is gain. The contract price is what the seller *gets* as opposed to the selling price, which is the total the buyer will *pay* including mortgage assumed.

3. Now let's suppose the existing mortgage on the property is greater than *A*'s adjusted basis. Illustratively, *A* purchased the property he's selling to *B* for $20,000. The property, for first one reason and then another, substantially appreciated in value, and subsequent to his purchase of it, *A* borrowed $30,000 secured by a first mortgage. Now let's hypothesize that he sells the land for $160,000 to *B*, who pays $20,000 cash, assumes the existing $30,000 mortgage, and gives *A* a secured note for $110,000. Thus, we have cash of $20,000, a new note and mortgage of $110,000, and excess of the first mortgage over seller's basis ($30,000 over $20,000) of $10,000, a total of $140,000. Payments in the year of sale, then, are computed as cash—$20,000—*plus* excess of mortgage over *A*'s basis—$10,000—for a total of $30,000.

You might never have the kind of problem faced by the taxpayer in the third example, but in view of the dramatic valuation increase which it supposes, you might be pleased if you did.

Conceivably, the excess of mortgage over basis might defeat an installment sale, and thus one should be wary when treading in these waters. For example, suppose that *A*'s basis is $25,000 and his existing mortgage $30,000 at time of sale. He sells to *B* for $100,000—with $30,000 in cash at the front, assumption of the existing mortgage, and a new second paper of $40,000. Note that here payments in the year of sale total $35,000 ($30,000 cash but $5,000 excess of first mortgage over basis). *A* is going to be chagrined to hear from the IRS at some later time that he really received 35 percent of the $100,000 sale price in the year of sale and thus that he has to pay the whole blooming tax (plus some penalty and interest, naturally) at one fell swoop, notwithstanding the fact that he hasn't yet received all of the sales price.

Another situation calling for surefootedness in installment sales is presented by the no-interest case. *A* might not want any interest on deferred income, so he simply prices his land at a higher figure than he otherwise might. *B* would rather pay interest (it's deductible to him) but, desiring the land mightily, goes along with this pricing formula. Let's say that *A*'s basis is $30,000 and that he sells for $48,000, taking 30 percent ($14,400) in cash at the front with the deferred balance of $33,600 payable in three subsequent annual installments of $11,200 each, the deferred amount to be without interest. Under the existing regulations, the IRS will consider this a tax-dodging effort on *A*'s part and will impute interest at the rate of 7 percent per annum. This means that a portion of the deferred payments will be treated as interest, thus increasing *A*'s percentage of principal received in the year of sale. In this instance, since *A*'s initial payment was exactly 30 percent of the sale price, even one cent of imputed interest in the $33,600 balance remaining would push *A* over the cliff. The IRS would tell *A* that instead of selling his land for $48,000, he had actually sold it for $43,557 and thus, instead of collecting 30 percent, had raked in 33 percent. Thus, though he must wait three years to collect his full sales price, he must pay the full tax bite immediately.

Again, I admonish you: Lean on your accountant or tax lawyer *before* firming a sales agreement. It's cheaper to pay these breeds early than to cry on their shoulders late.

Fifteen
Finale

Now that you have absorbed the preceding comments, and assuming you feel that a case has been made for investment in real estate, don't just sit there. Do something.

As an opening gambit, why not call a couple of friends and get together for a general discussion of the subject. Maybe over lunch. You will probably find that each of you has ideas concerning some prospective purchases, maybe ideas that you'd entertained for some time but lacked the savvy or financial strength to pursue.

Your first commitment of funds might be the $50 or so required to charter a small plane and pilot for an aerial tour of your town and its environs. No trip about a city is quite so revealing as one made in a low-flying aircraft. One perceives at a glance where the good action is and the growth potentials are, as well as where the area's environmental ills are or seem apt to soon be. Such a flight might only confirm what you've already observed from more pedestrian perspectives. Even if this is all you get, it will be nice to have your earlier judgment corroborated.

As well as doing your own aerial survey, you will also be able in most communities to take advantage of professional aerial mapping. Ask your local planning office if your county has been photographed in this fashion. If it has, you will most likely be able to purchase copies of map sections showing sites or areas in which you're particularly interested (going rate for this service in our county is $3 the sheet).

Don't let your age or financial status deter you. You can start at any time and play with any amount. Our original group was made up of individuals in their mid-forties, and our only regret is that we didn't start our program years sooner.

In the chapter titled "Going It Alone" we analyzed a $50,000 purchase, catalyzed with a $5,000 down payment. Purchase possibilities of comparable scope are all about you. If you want to wet your feet with an absolute minimum of initial exposure, why not shop for a well-located duplex or possibly a couple of row houses in a transforming neighborhood?

Far more important than the number of dollars you initially decide to invest is your commitment to pyramid. No path to wealth is always an easy one. You will be discouraged by occasional financing difficulties or general market doldrums or that long-standing vacancy, but don't lose your resolve. As you proceed, and in a shorter time period than you would probably have estimated, you will find your possessions multiplying and your problems—particularly the financial ones—easing. Don't weaken. Stack one property on another. If you can fashion your growth without departing from your original group, so much the better.

You'll find it's exciting to receive a deed with your partnership shown as new owner of the property described in it; that it's fun to drive by your own property, to see it being used, to know firsthand what's happening to your investment. I've just never had that feeling when buying stock, have never known what made my modest holdings rise or fall in value, have never been privy to what went on in the boardrooms of the large corporations I've owned small bits and pieces of. It's so different with landholding. You can walk on your turf, observe its dimensions, see and control what's happening there.

If your property is income-producing, you know that each day earns you a little more and that monthly the checks will come to your door. Even though you'll be forwarding a large portion of this income to your mortgagees, you will find comfort in the knowledge that with each such payment your equity increases and that your property values will be more influenced by inflationary trends than by deflationary ones in the national economy. Rents are far more apt to hold steady or to rise than to fall.

Make your first investment very carefully, and make unanimity a requisite of your group's decisions. In making your initial acquisition, if you can deal with people and property you're well acquainted with, you'll feel that much more secure. As you become more sophisticated, you will be able to rely with increasing confidence on your own collective judgment.

Don't be afraid to venture. For us, venturing is half the fun. Testing the flexibility of purchase (or sale) arrangements is exciting within itself. What's in the seller's mind? Does he really have two other prospects waiting in the wings, or is he bluffing in hopes of extracting a higher offer from you? Does "I don't care whether I sell or not" really mean "Make me an offer—any offer—quick"?

It's always easy to test the water. Before transmitting any proposal, you should have decided how far you will go. How far you will go will be determined by how much you want the property and, more important, by how supportive the income (or environment in the case of raw land) will be of your top price. Don't be afraid to counter a seller's asking price (if you believe it to be preposterously high) with an offer which—at least when matched against the seller's apparent value opinion—is preposterously low. To put it another way, with respect to any offer you submit anticipate that a seller might give an affirmative response. After all, he only has three choices: yes, no, and maybe.

Remember always that your own opinion of value is more important than the seller's. I repeat an earlier warning: Don't lose excellent investment opportunities through rigid application of the old notion that a seller will always take less than he asks. A seller might and a seller mightn't, but while you're hanging around waiting to see whether he will or won't—and if he will, how much less—an opportunist (i.e., one who recognizes a good buy when he sees it) may slip in and take it all away from you.

While there will always be good investment situations in real estate, you will not find them available at regular intervals or always when you're in quest of one. Thus, recognition of the genuine article becomes an important factor in real estate investing.

There is always present, in any land transaction, the feeling—usually short-lived but sometimes recurring—that you have done the wrong thing. But, believe me, if you have stayed fairly close to the guidelines set out in this book, these momentary and sporadic concerns will vanish in the night.

You will have some headaches as you move toward becoming one of the landed gentry, but these will seem as nothing when you ride by your holdings and see them working steadily for you.

Well, I've gotten you this far. The rest of the way you're on your own. Check back in five or six years and let me know how things are going.

Appendixes

Legal requirements for contracts and other documents will vary from state to state. The following forms are simply samples of these kinds of documents but the reader would be well advised to check with an attorney before formalizing contractual undertakings of these kinds.

1.

NORTH CAROLINA)
                  :   PARTNERSHIP AGREEMENT
CENTER COUNTY)

THIS IS AN AGREEMENT, made and entered into
this 1st day of January, 1979, by and among ALBERT
BAKER, CHARLES DOGGETT, ELEANOR FRIEDMAN
and GEORGE HOWELL, all of Center County, North
Carolina.

W I T N E S S E T H:

WHEREAS the parties mutually desire to associate
themselves as a partnership for the purpose of acquiring, holding and developing real estate;

NOW, THEREFORE, the parties hereto agree for
themselves, their successors and assigns as follows:

1. *Name and Business.* The parties do hereby
form a partnership under the name of QUEENSLAND
SHOPPING CENTER, to acquire, hold and develop real
estate in North Carolina. The principal place of business of the partnership shall be located at 1400 South
Street, Center City, North Carolina, but the partnership
may establish additional places of business at other
locations either within or without the State of North
Carolina.

2. *Term.* The partnership shall begin on January
1, 1979, and shall continue until terminated as herein
provided.

3. *Capital.* The initial capital of the partnership
shall be contributed by the several partners in the ratio
hereinafter set forth in paragraph 4 for the sharing of
profits and losses of the partnership. In the event that
the cash funds of the partnership are not sufficient to
meet its operating expenses, the several partners shall

also make additional capital contributions to the partnership in the same ratio.

4. *Profit and Loss.* Subject to the provisions of paragraph 5, the net profits and net losses of the partnership shall be shared and borne by the partners in the following ratio:

ALBERT BAKER	25%
CHARLES DOGGETT	25%
ELEANOR FRIEDMAN	25%
GEORGE HOWELL	25%

5. *Compensation.* No compensation for services will be paid to any partner but this provision is subject to change by agreement among all the partners at any time. Any compensation paid shall in any event be deducted from partnership income, as in the case of any other expense, in determining the net profit or loss of the partnership distributable or chargeable to the partners.

6. *Management, Duties and Restrictions.* The partners shall have equal rights in the management of the partnership business, but Albert Baker is hereby appointed and designated as general manager of the partnership business and is hereby authorized to act for and on behalf of the partnership in all transactions arising in the ordinary course of the partnership business. No partner, however, without the consent of the other partners, shall on behalf of the partnership borrow or lend money or sell or contract to sell any property for or of the partnership other than the type of property bought, sold and handled in the regular course of the partnership business.

7. *Banking.* The River Bank, of Center City, North Carolina, is designated as a depository for the funds of the partnership, and all funds of the partnership

shall be deposited in its name in an account or accounts at such bank or at such other bank as may from time to time be designated by the partners. No withdrawal from the account of the partnership shall be made except by check or draft signed by at least two of the partners.

8. *Books.* The partnership books shall be maintained at the offices of Albert Baker, and each partner shall at all times have access thereto. The books shall be kept on a calendar year basis and shall be closed and balanced at the end of each calendar year.

9. *Voluntary Termination.* The partnership may be dissolved at any time by agreement of the partners and in such event the partners shall proceed with reasonable promptness to liquidate the business of the partnership.

10. *Retirement.* Any partner shall have the right to retire from the partnership at the end of any calendar year. Written notice of intention to retire shall be served upon the other partners at least three months before the end of the calendar year. The retirement of such partner shall have no effect upon the continuance of the partnership business. The remaining partners shall have the right to either purchase the retiring partner's interest in the partnership or to terminate and liquidate the partnership business. If the remaining partners elect to purchase the interest of the retiring partner, they shall serve written notice of such election upon the retiring partner within two months after receipt of the latter's notice of intention to retire and the purchase price and method of payment for the partnership interest shall be the same as hereinafter stated with reference to the purchase of a decedent's interest in the partnership. If the remaining partners do not elect to purchase the interest of the retiring partner in the partnership, the partners shall proceed with reason-

able promptness to liquidate the business of the partnership.

11. *Death.* In the event of the death of a partner, the business of the partnership shall be continued to the end of the calendar year in which such death occurs. The estate of the deceased partner shall share in the net profits or losses of the partnership for the balance of the calendar year in the same way the deceased partner would have shared in them had he survived to the end of the calendar year, but liability of the estate for losses shall not exceed the deceased partner's interest in the partnership assets at the time of his death. At the end of the calendar year, the surviving partners shall have the option either to liquidate the partnership or to purchase the interest of the deceased partner. Thereafter the estate of the deceased partner shall have no interest in the partnership and the surviving partners shall have the right to continue the business by themselves or with others without accounting for trade name, good will, or other intangible values.

(a) If the surviving partners elect to purchase the interest of the deceased partner, the purchase price shall be the fair market value of a one-fourth interest in the total equity of the partnership in any real estate owned by the partnership at the time of the death of the deceased partner. In the event the Executor of the estate of the deceased party and the surviving partners cannot agree as to what such fair market value is, then three disinterested appraisers shall make a determination of value and the parties agree to be bound by such determination. The surviving partners shall choose one appraiser, the representative of the deceased shall choose another and these two shall choose the third. By agreement among the parties, this method of valuation may be changed.

(b)   If the surviving partners do not elect to purchase the interest of the deceased partner, they shall proceed with reasonable promptness to liquidate the partnership. During the period of liquidation the surviving partners and the estate of the deceased partner shall share in the profits and losses of the business in the same way that they would have shared in them had the deceased partner survived to the end of the calendar year except that the deceased partner's estate shall not be liable for losses in excess of the deceased partner's interest in the partnership assets at the time of his death.

12.   *Assignment.* A partner, without the written consent of the other partners, shall not have any right to sell, assign, pledge or mortgage his interest in the partnership.

IN WITNESS WHEREOF, the parties hereto have affixed their hands and seals all as of the day and year first above written.

_____(SEAL)

ALBERT BAKER

_____(SEAL)

CHARLES DOGGETT

_____(SEAL)

ELEANOR FRIEDMAN

_____(SEAL)

GEORGE HOWELL

2.

NORTH CAROLINA)
                 :   O P T I O N
CENTER COUNTY)

THIS IS AN OPTION given this _____ day of June, 1978, by ROBERT CELLAR, of Center City, North Carolina, hereinafter called OPTIONOR, to WILL PROFFIT AND ASSOCIATES, a partnership with its principal office in Center City, North Carolina, hereinafter called OPTIONEE.

OPTIONOR, in consideration of the sum of Two Thousand Dollars ($2,000.00) received from OPTIONEE, receipt of which is hereby acknowledged, does by these presents give to OPTIONEE the exclusive option to purchase, upon the terms and conditions hereinafter set out, certain real property in Center County, more particularly described as follows:

[Insert description]

This option shall be effective through and including the 31st day of July, 1978. OPTIONEE may extend the option for an additional period extending through and including September 30, 1978, by paying to OPTIONOR an additional Two Thousand Dollars ($2,000.00), such payment to be made on or before July 15, 1978.

The purchase price for the property hereinabove described is Fifty Thousand Dollars ($50,000.00), against which there shall be credited the consideration paid for this option and any extension thereof. OPTIONEE will pay the balance of the purchase price at the time of purchase. He will pay in cash the difference between any moneys paid for options hereunder and Five Thousand Dollars ($5,000.00) and he will execute and deliver to the OPTIONOR a promissory note for the remaining Forty-Five Thousand Dollars ($45,000.00), secured by a mortgage encumbering the said real property, in form acceptable to the OPTIONOR. Such promissory note and mortgage will provide for payment of the remaining Forty-Five Thousand Dollars ($45,000.00) in nine (9) equal annual installments of Five Thousand ($5,000.00) each, together with interest thereon at the rate of eight per cent (8%) per annum, with interest on the unpaid amount payable with each installment of principal. OPTIONEE will pay costs incurred in connection with the preparation of such note and mortgage and the recording of the mortgage.

Upon receipt of the balance of the purchase price, OPTIONOR will promptly execute and deliver to OPTIONEE a good and sufficient deed, with proper documentary stamps affixed thereto, conveying the real property to the OPTIONEE and shall at the same time deliver possession of the property to the purchaser.

Real property taxes, insurance premiums on transferable policies and current rents from tenants will be prorated as of the date of closing.

All matters relating to this option, including the payment of the purchase price and delivery of the deed and of the note and mortgage, will take place at the office of Sooner and Later, Attorneys, Suite 200, Angel Building, Center City, North Carolina.

OPTIONOR warrants and represents that he has the authority to grant this option and that he holds a good fee simple marketable title to the property referred to herein. In the event OPTIONOR for any reason cannot convey a good title at such time as OPTIONEE exercises the right granted hereby, then OPTIONOR agrees that he will return to OPTIONEE any moneys paid under the terms of this instrument to OPTIONOR upon which payment neither party will have any further obligation to the other. In the event OPTIONOR refuses to return the money, notwithstanding his inability to convey a fee simple marketable title, thus compelling OPTIONEE to institute legal proceedings to recover such sums, OPTIONOR agrees that in the event OPTIONEE is successful in such litigation that OPTIONOR will pay reasonable attorneys' fees to OPTIONEE'S counsel as determined by a court of law having jurisdiction of the subject matter.

If the option is exercised and the property described herein purchased, OPTIONOR agrees that he will pay any real estate brokerage commissions which might have been incurred by reason of the sale.

All notices and other items required to be given or delivered under this option shall be sent to OPTIONOR at 400 West Street, Center City, North Carolina, and to OPTIONEE at 400 East Street, Center City, North Carolina.

IN WITNESS WHEREOF OPTIONOR has signed and acknowledged the execution of this option on this the day and year first above written.

_____(SEAL)
ROBERT CELLAR, Optionor

NORTH CAROLINA)
                         :
CENTER COUNTY)

I, _____, a Notary Public of _____ County, State of North Carolina, do hereby certify that ROBERT CELLAR personally appeared before me this day and acknowledged the execution of the foregoing option.

Witness my hand and notarial seal, this _____ day of _____, 197__.

_____

Notary Public

My commission expires:

_____

3.

NORTH CAROLINA)
:   OFFER TO PURCHASE REAL
      ESTATE
CENTER COUNTY   )

The undersigned WILL PROFFIT AND ASSOCIATES, a partnership, with its principal office in Center City, North Carolina, hereinafter referred to as OFFEROR, hereby offers to purchase from CREDITOR CORPORATION, a North Carolina company with its principal office in Center City, North Carolina, hereinafter referred to as OFFEREE, certain real estate located at 5000 Bingham Blvd. in Center City, and more particularly described as follows:

[Insert description]

OFFEROR agrees to pay the sum of Two Hundred Fifty Thousand Dollars ($250,000) for the said property, upon the following terms and conditions:

(1) OFFEROR understands that there is at present an assumable mortgage on the property in the approximate amount of One Hundred Fifty Thousand Dollars ($150,000) and as a part of the total purchase price OFFEROR would assume and agree to pay such mortgage. For the difference between the balance due on such mortgage and Two Hundred Twenty Thousand Dollars ($220,000), OFFEROR will give to OFFEREE at the time of closing a note and deed of trust, bearing interest at the rate of eight per cent (8%) per annum and payable in three (3) equal annual installments of principal and such interest as may be due at such annual anniversaries. OFFEROR will pay the remaining Thirty Thousand Dollars ($30,000) in cash at the

time of closing. As an earnest of its good faith, OF-FEROR transmits herewith Two Thousand Five Hundred Dollars ($2,500) to be applied against the total purchase price as a credit. If the offer is accepted, OFFEROR would owe an additional Twenty-Seven Thousand Five Hundred Dollars ($27,500) in cash at time of closing.

(2)   Current leases affecting the subject property must be assignable and assigned to OFFEROR at the time of closing.

(3)   In addition to being able to assign leases with current tenants, OFFEREE must also be able to convey a good fee simple, marketable insurable title, subject only to existing restrictions of record, easements for public utilities and driveways, applicable zoning ordinances and the mortgage hereinabove referred to. If, subject only to the recited exceptions, OFFEREE is unable to convey a good fee simple, marketable title, it will on demand of OFFEROR return the Two Thousand Five Hundred Dollars ($2,500) submitted herewith. If OFFEREE can, subject only to the recited exceptions, convey a good fee simple title but OFFEROR does not elect to consummate the sale—notwithstanding OF-FEREE's acceptance of the offer transmitted hereby—then OFFEREE may retain the Two Thousand Five Hundred Dollar ($2,500) payment as liquidated damages and shall not be entitled to further payment by way of damages or otherwise from OFFEROR.

(4)   All taxes and assessments which may have become a lien upon the described real estate at the date of closing will be paid by OFFEREE. Insurance premiums, interest, rents or water bills, ad valorem taxes, bulk fuels, and any other benefits or burdens, whether herein mentioned or not, which are directly related to the cost of maintaining and operating the property hereinabove described shall be prorated and

adjusted to the date of closing. OFFEREE shall make payments on the existing mortgage through and including the last month for which such payments are due before the closing date. Closing will be on the first day of October, 1979, at such Center City location as OFFEREE may select.

(5) All notices given or made in connection with this offer will be deemed sufficient if in writing and mailed to OFFEROR or OFFEREE at the addresses shown below.

WILL PROFFIT AND ASSOCIATES,
a partnership, OFFEROR

By:_____

ACCEPTANCE

The foregoing offer of Will Proffit and Associates is hereby accepted subject to the terms and conditions hereinabove set out. OFFEREE acknowledges receipt of the deposit money transmitted with the offer.

Done on this _____ day of August, 1979.

CREDITOR CORPORATION

By: _____

4.

NORTH CAROLINA)
             :   AGREEMENT OF SALE
CENTER COUNTY)

THIS IS AN AGREEMENT OF SALE made and entered into this 1st day of January, 1979, by and between WILL PROFFIT AND ASSOCIATES, a partnership with its principal office in Center City, North Carolina, hereinafter referred to as BUYER, and ELIZABETH ATKINS PARSONS, a resident of Center County, North Carolina, hereinafter referred to as SELLER.

In consideration of the agreements herein contained, the parties do agree as follows:

(1) SELLER agrees to sell and convey and BUYER to purchase and take title to that certain parcel of real estate lying and being located in Center County, North Carolina, consisting of approximately two (2) acres of land together with all improvements thereon, known as Parsons Apartments, and more particularly described in the attached Exhibit "A" which is incorporated herein by reference.

(2) BUYER will pay to SELLER a total of Four Hundred Thousand Dollars ($400,000) for the said property, payment to be made at the time of closing and in the following manner:

(a) Fifty Thousand Dollars ($50,000) will be paid in cash and Three Hundred Fifty Thousand Dollars ($350,000) will be paid by a note in the face amount of Three Hundred Fifty Thousand Dollars ($350,000) bearing interest at the rate of nine per cent (9%) per annum and payable in equal monthly installments over a period of twenty-five (25) years, said monthly installments of principal and interest to be in the amount of Two Thousand Nine Hundred Thirty-Seven and 20/100 Dollars ($2,937.20), the final payment to be in such amount as may then be due. On the tenth anniversary of such note, the SELLER or her assigns may at her or their option demand that the full balance of the note then due be paid. SELLER or her assigns will give BUYER ninety (90) days' written notice of her or their intention to exercise such option. In the event the option is not exercised, then the note shall continue payable in accordance with its terms. BUYER or BUYER's assigns shall, however, at any time during the life of the note, have the right to prepay the same in full without penalty. Payment of the note herein described will be secured by a purchase money mortgage on the property in favor of the SELLER.

(3) This transaction will be closed by delivery of a properly executed general warranty deed to BUYER and delivery to SELLER of the moneys and documents hereinabove mentioned (and upon performance of all other obligations imposed by this agreement on the part of both parties) at the offices of SELLER's attorneys, HURRI AND WAITE, Suite 300, Lawyers Building, Center City, North Carolina, on April 1, 1979. SELLER warrants that she will be able to convey a good, marketable, insurable fee simple title to the property subject only to public utilities easements as the same appear of record and 1979 taxes which will be prorated between the parties as of the date of closing. If title examination by BUYER reveals a defect in the title held by SELLER, BUYER will immediately notify SELLER of such discovery and SELLER will have thirty (30) days within which to remedy the same and in the event the said thirty-day period falls at such time as to go beyond the closing date herein set, then the time for closing shall be extended but in no event, absent a contrary agreement by the parties, shall such extension exceed the time required for the thirty-day period to run its course.

(4) BUYER shall have the privilege of going on the property prior to closing for surveys and other studies and agrees to hold SELLER harmless from any damages which might result from such visitation. BUYER agrees that it will pay any survey expenses incurred and will advise any surveyor retained by BUYER to this effect in advance of surveyor's going upon the property.

(5) SELLER will be responsible for all assessments due and payable prior to and at the time of closing.

(6) In the event the property herein described is damaged by fire or other casualty prior to closing, SELLER shall have the option to restore the property to as good a condition as existed prior to such casualty. If SELLER fails to so restore in a reasonable time, BUYER may void this agreement, receiving a refund of any moneys advanced, or by agreement with SELLER complete the transaction of purchase and sale under an assignment of any insurance proceeds payable by reason of such damage or loss from SELLER to BUYER. SELLER agrees to maintain existing casualty, fire and extended loss insurance coverage on the property until closing and to pay her prorata portion of the annual cost of such coverage through the closing date.

(7) The parties hereto recognize that if BUYER defaults in its obligations hereunder, the question of determining SELLER's damages would be difficult and therefore it is agreed that BUYER's liability in the event of such default will be limited to earnest moneys paid contemporaneously with the execution of this agreement in the amount of Five Thousand Dollars ($5,000) and that BUYER shall have no further liability to SELLER on account of any claims which might arise out of such breach.

(8) All available contractor's, manufacturer's and dealer's warranties and guaranties affecting improvements, equipment and fixtures located on the property,

including but not by way of limitation air conditioning and heating systems, refrigerators, stoves, washers, dryers, garbage disposals and all other utility warranties, if any, shall be assigned by SELLER to BUYER at the time of closing.

(9) Within seven (7) days from the execution of this agreement, SELLER will forward to BUYER a list of tenants of the apartments located on the property described herein, together with a statement of taxes and insurance paid for 1978 and utility bills paid for the same period. SELLER will further provide BUYER with an itemized list of all personal property to be conveyed at the time of closing as well as with written assurance that there are no claims or liens against the said items.

(10) SELLER agrees to prorate as of the date of closing rentals and other income from leases and to transfer all funds pertaining to the property in its escrow account to the BUYER in closing. If there have been collections for security or other tenant trust deposits and these have not been separately maintained in an escrow account, there will be an adjustment in the purchase price at closing to cover these deposits collected but not escrowed.

(11) SELLER warrants to BUYER that SELLER has no knowledge of any pending condemnation proceedings against the property or any part thereof; that SELLER is not a party to any litigation affecting the property or any part thereof; and that there are no liens filed against the property or any part thereof, nor any violations of building codes or zoning ordinances and that air conditioning, heating systems and other mechanical equipment are in good working order.

(12) SELLER warrants that there is no management contract that will continue beyond the time of purchase by BUYER. SELLER acknowledges receipt of Five Thou-

sand Dollars ($5,000) paid to her contemporaneously with the execution of this agreement, which amount will be applied to the purchase price at time of closing, reducing the cash balance due to Forty-Five Thousand Dollars ($45,000).

This agreement constitutes the entire undertaking between the parties. It shall enure to the benefit of and be binding upon the parties and their heirs, successors and assigns.

BUYER will be permitted to take possession from SELLER at the time of closing.

IN WITNESS WHEREOF, the parties hereto have set their hands and seals, the day and year first above written.

WILL PROFFIT AND ASSOCIATES,
a partnership

By:_____
    BUYER

_____(SEAL)
ELIZABETH ATKINS PARSONS, SELLER

Index

index

Index

Accelerated depreciation, 15, 109, 172–175
  (See also Depreciation)
Accountants, 34–35
Ad valorem taxes, 9, 65, 121, 138
Add-on building permit, 122
Advertising, 39–40, 44
Aerial survey, 179–180
Ambiguities in written documents, 158
Amortization period, 25
Anchor tenants, 69
Apartment property, 14, 16, 90–101, 119, 120
  depreciation benefits, 94, 95
  leases, 152
  management of, 93–94
  valuation of, 91–92
Appraisers, 54, 155, 163, 171
  government, 154, 155
Arby's, 102, 105, 113
Athens, Greece, 42

Balloon financing, 127–128, 130, 132
Bank loan officers, 36
Bankers, 77, 84, 128–130
Banking, 35–36
Bankrupt debtors, 46
Banks, 36, 50, 77, 129
Base rent, 69–72, 110, 112, 134
Basis, 167
Bathrooms in office buildings, 121–122
Black's legal dictionary, 2
Bonds, 1, 13
Brokers, 13, 122, 150
  defined, 37n
  fee of, 38, 123–124
  and finding property, 38–39
Building-code, 18
  for bathrooms, 121–122
Building-life estimates, 15, 170
Built-up equity, 109
Bureau of Labor Statistics, 121
Burger King, 113

Business property, 14–16, 91, 169
  buying of, 64–89
    calculating yield, 82–87
    cash flow and tax benefits, 87–89
    financing of, 68–71
    formulating your offer, 71–78
    making an offer, 78–81
  depreciation of, 94
  leases for, 152
  vs. residential property, 90
  value of, 18
  (See also Income-producing property; Property)

Capital gains tax, 33, 57, 59, 73, 109, 150, 167–168
Capital losses, 167–168
Capital transactions, tax consequences of, 166–178
Capitalization rate and rent multiples, 91–92
Cash flow in business property, 87–89
Center city, 41–43
Central business district (CBD), 45
Chambers of commerce, 41, 43
Charles II, 23
Clerks of court, 3
Closing, 25, 55
Commercial land users, 52
Commercial property, 149
  leases for, 152
  (See also Business property; Income-producing property; Property)
Commercial transactions, 75
Commissions of brokers, 38, 123–124
Company-owned stores, 103
Compensating balance, 141
Condemnation proceedings, 54, 152–158, 168
Condemnation law, 158
Condominiums, price of, 55
"Consideration," 78
Constitution and just compensation, 154, 155

Construction, 20, 102, 106
  costs of, 41
  of franchises, 107–109
Contract of sale, 24, 25, 55, 80
Corporate tax, 27
Corporation, 27–28
Cost-of-living escalator, 111
Cost-of-living index, 121
County planning office, 11, 80
Credit standing, 129

Death
  intestate, 2
  of partners, 31, 33
  testate, 2
Debt, liability for in limited partner-
    ship, 30
Declining balance method, 172–173
Deeds
  recording of, 3–4
  restrictive covenants in, 20
  of transfer, 2
  of trust, 4
Deferred income, 150
Deficiency judgments, 62
Depletion, 170
Depreciation, 12, 13, 27, 29, 30, 34
  accelerated, 15, 109, 172–175
  on apartment property, 94, 95
  on buildings, 14–15
  on income-producing property, 89
  tax consequences of, 169–176
Depreciation allowance, 169–170
Depreciation schedules, 172–174
Depression, 62
Developers, 51, 52
Devisees, 2
Direct financing, 162
Discounting paper, 147
Displaced tenant, 154
Downtown, 41–45

Earnest money, 23, 81
Easement, 156
Elevators, 43
Eminent domain, 152, 168
  of utility companies, 156–157
Energy crisis, 42
England, 1, 2
Equity growth, 33
Equity and income property, 12

Equity value, 130
Escrow, 59–61

Fair market value of land, 155
  defined, 7
Farmland, value of, 18
Fast-food franchises, 102, 103,
    105–107, 111, 113, 116
Federal funds, 154
Federal tax laws, 27
Fee, 2
Fee simple, 2
Feoffments, 2
Feud, 2
Financing
  and banks, 35–36
  business property, 68–77
  direct, 162
  of income property, 13, 14
  of land, 5–7
  long-term, 13, 14, 50, 136
  of non-income-producing land, 10
  permanent, 134, 136, 137
  personal, 147
  of raw land, 56–63
  of shopping centers, 69
  short-term, 35, 49, 50
Fixed rent, 111, 149
Florence, Italy, 42
Forced sales, 46–47
Foreclosure, 62, 115
  and deeds of trust, 4
Fort Lauderdale, 6
Franchises, 102–118
  construction of, 107–109
  leasing to, 103–107
Front money, 25

Government, 14, 166
  appraisers, 154
  and eminent domain, 152, 178
  and land ownership, 10
  subsidized programs of, 94
Grantee, 2
Grantor, 2
Gross rents, 71
Gross sales approach, 110
Ground leasing, 111–113, 115, 117
Group investment, 9, 26, 159
  formation of group, 31–34

Index 207

Houses, price of, 55

Income-producing property, 12–17,
21, 27, 47, 48, 66, 89, 109, 115,
165, 169, 181
and record keeping, 34
selling of, 148–151
value of, 51
(See also Apartment property;
Business property; Commer-
cial property; Property)
Income tax, 29–30, 89, 151
Incompetency proceedings, 5
Incorporation, 27
Industrial property, value of, 18
Industrial Revolution, 1
Inflation and depreciation, 172
In-house management rules, 31
Installment sales, 57, 60–61, 73, 74,
109, 150
tax consequences of, 176–178
Institutional borrowing, 163
Insurance companies, 50, 68
Insurance costs, 47
Interest, 29, 30, 34, 61, 69, 112
rates of, 73
on raw land, 52–53
and second mortgages, 76
Internal Revenue Code
and depreciation, 169
subchapter S, 27
Internal Revenue Service, 15, 27, 60,
89, 109, 130
and depreciation, 170, 171
Interstate exit locations, 53, 107
Involuntary conversion, 168–169

Joint ownership, 26
Judgment, 5
Judgment debtors, 46
"Just compensation," 154

Kentucky Fried Chicken, 103, 105,
113

Land
and depreciation, 170
income-producing, 12–17
marketing advantages and disadvantages, 7–8
non-income-producing, 8–11

ownership
how to come by, 1–3
records of, 3–5
types of, 26–31
uniqueness and financeability of,
5–7, 24
(See also Land values; Property;
Raw land)
Land-development business, 21
Land leasing
leasing from, 111–115
leasing to, 110–111
Land values
and franchises, 105–106
income-producing land, 12, 51
non-income-producing land, 8–9
raw land, 53–56
and zoning categories, 18
Land titles, 2, 3
Land transfers, 2
Large transactions, 133–142
Lawyers, 34–35
Lease, 12, 48, 50, 68–70, 134, 152
for apartments, 194
and condemnation, 153, 154
for office buildings, 120–121
Lease strength, 68
Leasehold interest, 24
Leasehold value, 153
Leasing of land, 110–115
Letter transaction, 78
advantages of, 81
Life span of buildings, 15, 170
Limited partnerships, 30
Liquidated damage clause, 62
"Livery of seisin," 2
Local opportunities for investment,
40–41
Long John Silver's, 102
Long-term amortization schedule,
127
Long-term capital gain, 167
Long-term financing, 50, 136
of income property, 13, 14
Long-term leases, 68, 69
Long-term lenders, 68

McDonald's, 102, 103, 105, 113
Maintenance costs, 47
Management of apartments, 93–94

Maps
  aerial, 180
  tax assessors, 40, 64–65
Margin requirements, 55
Market value, defined, 54
Maryland, 24
Master Appraisal Institute, 171
Merchants' associations, 43
Metes and bounds description, 46
Monaco, 6
Mortgages, 46, 73
  guaranty insurance for, 13
  recording of, 4
Multi-family land, 90–101
  value of, 18
  (See also Apartment property)

Naked loss, 167
Net, net, net formula, 104, 112
New York, 24
No-interest case, 178
Non-income-producing land, 8–11
  (See also Land; Property; Raw
    land)
North Carolina, 23
North Carolina Real Estate Licen-
  sing Board, 37n

Office buildings, 119–132
Older buildings, 16, 41–43, 95, 123
Options, 23–25, 47–50, 55, 80, 163
Overages, 68–71, 87, 133, 137, 140,
  149, 159
Ownership of land
  how to come by, 1–3
  records of, 3–5
  types of
    corporation, 27–28
    partnership, 29–31
    tenancy in common, 28–29
    trust, 29

Partition proceedings, 46
Partnership, 27–31, 33
Patron security, 103
Percentage allocation of value, 171
Percentage override clause, 104
Permanent financing, 134, 136, 137
Personal financing, 147
Personal investment program,
  159–165

Pizza Hut, 102
Planning office, 11, 80
Power of attorney, 28
Preliminary evaluation of property,
  47–48
Pricing of raw land, 11, 53–56
Principal, deferring payment of, 61
Property
  assessments, 9
    (See also Ad valorem taxes)
  commercial, 149
  finding of, 37–47
    advertising, 39–40
    bargains, 45–47
    brokers, 27–28
    downtown, 41–45
    local opportunities, 40–41
  rights, 1
  steps after finding, 47–50
    option agreement, 48–50
    preliminary evaluation, 47–48
  taxes, 47, 71, 74
  values, 181
  (See also Apartment property;
    Business property; Commer-
    cial property; Income-pro-
    ducing property; Land; Land
    values; Non-income-produc-
    ing property)
Public record, 4, 5
Public registry, 4, 31, 48, 52
Public services, costs of, 42
Purchase-money mortgages, 14, 62,
  116
Pyramiding, 6, 95

Quid pro quo, 23
Quitclaim deed, 59

Railroad companies, 2
Raw land, 8–12, 21, 27, 34, 107, 149,
  151, 165, 182
  buying of, 51–63
    financing, 56–63
    pricing, 11, 53–56
  selling of, 143–147
  (See also Land; Non-income-pro-
    ducing land)
Real estate (see Land; Property)

Real estate agents, 146
  and deposit ethics, 146
  (See *also* Brokers)
Real estate fee, 144
Record keeping, 3, 34
Recording office, 3
Refinancing, 109
Registers of deeds, 3, 31
Release pricing, 58–61, 107, 144
Rent escalation formula, 69
Rent multiple, 91, 92
Rents, 12, 48, 68, 181
Residential property, 12
  multi-family, 18, 90–101
Resort property, 21–22
Restrictive covenants, 20
Retail business, 14
Retail property, value of, 74
Retail rental, 72
Risk in investment, 33–34
Rule Against Perpetuities, 158

Sales agreements, 23–25, 49, 50, 178
Sales-percentage overrides, 12
Sales-percentage rent clauses, 70
Savings and loan institutions, 13, 50,
  68, 75, 163
  and apartment property, 95
Second loan, 76
Second mortgage, 76, 150, 151
Securities transactions, 55
Security deposit, 94
"Seisin," 2, 3
Selling
  and depreciation, 174–176
  income property, 148–151
  raw land, 143–147
Sewer services, 11
Sharecropping tenants, 1
Shopping center, 41, 68, 119, 120
  financing of, 69
Short-term capital gain, 167
Short-term financing, 35, 49, 50
Short-term leases, 70
Signatory requirements for checks,
  31
Single-use buildings, 102–118
Society of Real Estate Appraisers,
  171
Statutes of frauds, 23

Straight-line depreciation, 172,
  174–175
Stockholders, 27, 28, 31
Stocks, 1, 13
Stores
  in center city, 41
  company-owned, 103
Subchapter S corporations, 27–28
Subordination, 115–118
Suburbia, 41, 42
Sum of the digits method, 172–174
Survey, value of, 55
Swaps of property, 169
Syndicate of partners, 30

Tax
  ad valorem, 9, 65, 121, 138
  on buildings, 14–15
  capital gains, 33, 57, 59, 73, 109,
    150
  consequences of buying and sell-
    ing, 166–178
    depreciation, 169–176
    gains and losses, 167–168
    installment sales, 176–178
    involuntary conversion, 168–169
    swaps, 169
  corporate, 27
  on downtown property, 45
  on income, 29–30, 89, 151
  on property, 47, 71, 74
  proration of, 50
  on raw land, 52–53
  and trusts, 29
Tax assessor's office, 40, 45, 52, 64
Tax benefits in business property,
  87–89
Tax collectors, 3
Tax escalation, 71
Tax escalator, 121
Tax laws, federal, 27
Tax liens, 5, 46
Tax Reform Act of 1976, 104, 109
Tax returns
  and partnerships, 29–30
  and tenancy in common, 28
Tax shelters, 14, 27, 51, 66, 149
Tax values, 54
Tenancy in common, 26, 28–29
Tenants, 69, 93–95, 154

Time financing, 147
Title insurance, 5
Title search, 50
  importance of, 5
Town-house unit, 92
"Tradearound," 169
Trading name, 29
Triple net lease, 104, 112
Trustees, 29
Trust agreements, 29
Trust ownership, 27
Trusts and downtown properties,
  44–45
Two hundred percent method, 173

Uniform Relocation Act, 154
United States, zoning in, 17
Urban-core revival, 42

Utility companies and eminent domain, 156–157, 168
Utility lines, 41

Vacancy factor, 88
Value appreciation potential, 51

Warranty deed, 5
Water services, 11
"Wraparound" obligations, 76, 84

Yield on business property,
  calculation of, 82–87

Zoning, 17–20
Zoning law, 18
Zoning office, 11